Entrepreneurial Innovation and Leadership

Nancy Richter • Paul Jackson
Thomas Schildhauer
Editors

Entrepreneurial Innovation and Leadership

Preparing for a Digital Future

palgrave
macmillan

Editors
Nancy Richter
Alexander von Humboldt Institute for
Internet and Society
Berlin, Germany

Paul Jackson
Edith Cowan University
Joondalup, WA
Australia

Thomas Schildhauer
Alexander von Humboldt Institute for
Internet and Society
Berlin, Germany

ISBN 978-3-319-71736-4   ISBN 978-3-319-71737-1   (eBook)
https://doi.org/10.1007/978-3-319-71737-1

Library of Congress Control Number: 2018934318

This Palgrave Pivot imprint is published by Springer Nature
The registered company is Springer International Publishing AG
The registered company address is: Gewerbestrasse 11, 6330 Cham, Switzerland

PREFACE

Germany is an innovation powerhouse—at least according to the Global Innovation Index (2015) and the OECD Science, Technology and Industry Scoreboard (2015). Good news, one would think, as relentless product turnover, Internet-mediated services and disruptive business models mean that without innovation a country cannot remain competitive and flourish. But although the country may be performing well in incremental innovation, *entrepreneurship* and the establishment of disruptive new businesses is another story. The volume of new business startups, including creative and agile young Internet startups, is surprisingly low in Germany. Why might this be the case? Is Germany resting on its industrial laurels, or are there other reasons: a conservative culture or poorly designed government policies, perhaps?

In contrast, the United States has very high rates of new business grounding, a model which Germany is now interested in emulating. American Internet startups such as Google, Amazon, Uber and Airbnb bring a continuous stream of new ideas and products onto the market and are disrupting existing industries to their core. We are of the view that Germany needs to achieve a better balance between incremental and radical innovation in order to secure its industrial and economic future.

One solution is for Germany to become more supportive of entrepreneurs and Internet startups. Currently, the most active startup scene is in Berlin, which has attractive living conditions and a growing network of investors, startups and innovative enterprises. Nevertheless, startups struggle: we need to understand why and strengthen the supportive conditions which increase the chances of success. This requires understanding the specific nature of the startup environment, as conventional factors associated with new business establishment do not yet come into play. For startups, the shape of the business model, the right team and the right competencies, savvy market knowledge and sales strategies that scale are also important. We need to look at the situation as a whole in order to observe the interactions between these contextual factors and identify what will help early-phase startups.

We should also consider how Germany might renew its established industries through radical innovation and by combining its existing capabilities with new ideas and directions. One pathway to greater balance for the German innovation system might lie in collaboration between the 'Old' and the 'New' economy. Increasingly, enterprises are working with innovative young companies in so-called 'accelerators', in which the entrepreneurs receive support in the form of expertise, mentoring, accommodation or financing for a limited period, usually a few months. The enterprises, seeking to boost their own innovation performance, gain fresh ideas and can absorb different ways of working by collaborating with these teams. This sounds like the perfect win–win scenario for the companies involved and for Germany, but the reality is more complex, and being successful needs high levels of mutual understanding, tolerance of differences, transparent interactions and project management processes, as well as clearly assigned organisational responsibilities.

In this edited book we take the themes of entrepreneurship, innovation and collaboration and seek some answers to the urgent question of how to make these collaborations work better. In the first chapter, Richter, Jackson and Schildhauer examine innovation in Germany and the USA and identify possible causes for the significant differences between them. Here it becomes clear that Germany performs worse than the USA in entrepreneurship, but must find its own solutions to encouraging greater startup and new venture activity. In Chap. 2, Richter, Volquartz, Schildhauer and Neumann identify and analyse the barriers and facilitators of new business grounding in Berlin. Then, in Chaps. 3, 4, 5 and 6, the most important building blocks in the new venture establishment process are illuminated: legal aspects, financing, business models, human resources and marketing. As an introduction, Richter and Schildhauer describe Startup Clinics, a practical research programme established at the Alexander von Humboldt Institute for Internet and Society (HIIG) in Berlin, which was designed to help startups by means of workshops and expert advice, but which also gathered and evaluated the resulting data.

This has led to the initiation of new and important research projects into Internet startups. Von Grafenstein pursues the question of how startups deal with complex data protection legislation governing data usage disclosures. Innovation processes are not straightforward, and it is difficult to specify in advance all purposes of data collection from users. However, this is basically required pursuant to the dominant view on the current legislation. In Chap. 5, Wrobel examines the competencies needed by successful entrepreneurial leaders. Marketing and sales are front and centre here, as these are the drivers of growth. In Chap. 6, Tech discusses the types of funding that startups should consider in the early phases of development and what they should consider when seeking investors, before going on to describe the current situation in Berlin. In Chap. 7, Dopfer underscores the significance of the business model for startups. This is a relatively underresearched topic, even though the business model is clearly fundamental in the establishment of a successful venture. Startups, particularly in the early stages, often have great difficulties in defining the right business model. This choice of business model is very often influenced by the particular background of the entrepreneur, so Dopfer presents ways in which startups can approach this more systematically and objectively.

Chapters 8, 9 and 10 turn their attention to the question of collaboration between established firms and startups, and what should be attended to in order to make these collaborations lead to successful innovation. First, Jackson, Richter and Schildhauer describe the barriers and propose methods by which established firms can increase the chance of successful outcomes. Subsequently, these authors discuss corporate accelerator programmes, a concrete solution to the challenge of bringing these organisations together for the purpose of boosting innovation. Finally, the authors discuss the different agile innovation processes that firms can take to increase radical innovation, and present examples and their respective benefits.

This book is directed at managers of organisations that are innovative or considering becoming more innovative in the face of changes and emerging threats in their marketplaces. It is also of interest to startups, as well as students, teachers and researchers into the increasingly important and contemporary theme of open innovation such as that occurring between established firms and startups. We also believe policymakers will be interested in understanding the role of startups and accelerators within the national innovation system.

This collection brings together the results of a long-standing collaboration between members of an international and cross-disciplinary research team. The analysis and the results are practical, useful and based upon rigorous research methods and sound theory. We hope readers will better understand radical innovation and entrepreneurship and be able to apply the findings to improve practice.

Alexander von Humboldt Institute for   Nancy Richter
Internet and Society, Berlin, Germany

Edith Cowan University,   Paul Jackson
Joondalup, WA, Australia

Alexander von Humboldt Institute for   Thomas Schildhauer
Internet and Society, Berlin, Germany

CONTENTS

Notes on Contributors

Martina Dopfer has been a researcher at the Alexander von Humboldt Institute for Internet and Society (HIIG) since 2014 and organises Startup Clinics for Business Model Innovation in collaboration with the Berlin-based Factory. Martina has a BA in Cultural and Communication Management from Zeppelin University, Friedrichshafen (Germany) and an MA in Management and Consulting from Lancaster University (UK). Martina gained her professional experience in various areas and companies worldwide.

Paul Jackson is a senior lecturer in the School of Business and Law and an associate researcher at HIIG. He is an information systems, knowledge and project management specialist who has been a systems developer, product development manager and project director, strategic consultant and university lecturer during an international career.

Konstanze Neumann joined the HIIG in 2013. She supports the Innovation and Entrepreneurship research project in the field of Internet-enabled innovation. She has studied Media and Communication Science at the University of Leipzig (Germany). Currently she is finishing a degree in Social and Cultural Anthropology and Political Science at Freie Universität Berlin.

Nancy Richter Since March 2014, Nancy Richter has been associate researcher at HIIG in the area of Innovation and Entrepreneurship. She completed her PhD at the Bauhaus-Universität Weimar (Germany), and deepened her studies at the University of St Andrews (Scotland) and at Edith Cowan University in Perth (Australia).

Thomas Schildhauer Since 2012, Thomas Schildhauer has been one of the executive directors of the HIIG, where he is responsible for the research topic Internet-based innovation. Since 2000 he has worked as a lecturer at the University of St Gallen (Switzerland). Further international experience was gained by visiting and working on research projects at the Massachusetts Institute of Technology, Boston (USA).

Robin Tech is principal investigator of a research group that focuses on the entrepreneurial exploitation of the 'Internet of things'. Prior to this, he studied Economics and Corporate Management at Zeppelin University (BA), Technology, Sociology & Management (MSc) in Stockholm (Sweden) and did his MBA in Hong Kong. In his non-academic life, Robin is the co-founder of AtomLeap, a high-tech-focused startup accelerator.

Lucie Volquartz is a media and startup professional currently working for Axel Springer SE. Prior to this, she worked on the startup team of Germany's leading digital association Bitkom, advocating for entrepreneurs' interests, as well as for different startups and in consulting. She is especially passionate about female entrepreneurship and co-founded Venture Ladies, a network for women in the startup and venture capital ecosystem.

Max von Grafenstein is head of the research programme Actors, Data and Infrastructures at HIIG. He is also a lawyer and runs the legal tech startup Innovation and Law, which focuses on privacy- and security-by-design solutions, data protection certificates, codes of conduct and binding corporate rules.

Martin Wrobel is a researcher at HIIG who has been working in the area of Internet-enabled innovation since 2013. Since October 2017, he has been a Visiting Professor of Marketing at the Berlin School of Economics and Law. His PhD research focused on individual competency requirements for founders in the sales and marketing role of an Internet-enabled startup.

LIST OF FIGURES

LIST OF TABLES

CHAPTER 1

Entrepreneurial Behaviour and Startups: The Case of Germany and the USA

Nancy Richter, Paul Jackson, and Thomas Schildhauer

Abstract Entrepreneurship is crucially important for the introduction of disruptive and radical innovation. However, in Germany entrepreneurship and disruptive innovation are consistently low whereas the USA, for example, performs very well in these areas. This chapter offers insights into the relevance of entrepreneurship for a national innovation system. It illustrates the effects of policy interventions on potential entrepreneurs and shows pathways to encourage entrepreneurial behaviour and startups.

Keywords Entrepreneurial behaviour • National Innovation System • Germany • USA • Radical innovation • Incremental innovation

N. Richter (✉) • T. Schildhauer
Alexander von Humboldt Institute for Internet and Society,
Berlin, Germany

P. Jackson
Edith Cowan University, Joondalup, WA, Australia

© The Author(s) 2018
N. Richter et al. (eds.), *Entrepreneurial Innovation and Leadership*,
https://doi.org/10.1007/978-3-319-71737-1_1

Entrepreneurship and Innovation at the National Level

Within the framework of a national innovation system (NIS),[1] startups are a source of new ventures, products and services and therefore a crucial driver of innovation, economic development and renewal. The German government regards startup businesses as an important source of economic growth (Audretsch, Dohse, & Niebuhr, 2009) and has initiated multiple programmes to encourage entrepreneurial behaviour (e.g. EXIST scholarships or, since 2015, ERP Venture Capital Fund investments for growth or follow-up financing). According to the Berlin Investmentbank (IBB), in Berlin a new startup is founded every 20 hours (IBB, 2017/2018). The multitude of startup events and the rise of incubators illustrate the increasing professionalism of the Berlin startup ecosystem. The rest of Germany is a different story, however: the rate of new business establishment in the country is consistently low (Jackson, Dobson, & Richter, 2017).

These numbers are worrying because startups are new market entrants that are very often responsible for radical and disruptive innovations (Ahuja & Lampert, 2001; Schumpeter, 1994). Radical and disruptive innovation is important for the long-term success of a NIS because it provides technologies, business models and rapid growth in new areas, and therefore supports a country's competitiveness (Jackson, Runde, Dobson, & Richter, 2015).

Recent reports by Cornell University, INSEAD, and the World Intellectual Property Organization (WIPO, an agency of the United Nations) (Cornell University, INSEAD, & WIPO, 2015), the Organisation for Economic Co-operation and Development (OECD 2015a, c) and the Global Entrepreneurship Monitor (Kelley, Singer, & Herrington, 2015) show that Germany performs well in innovation but poorly in entrepreneurship. The performance has even decreased over the past few years.

Political interventions should create supportive conditions that enable the emergence and expansion of startups. However, policymakers need comprehensive information about entrepreneurial behaviour to develop effective policy initiatives. This guide explains the relevance of innovation in startups to the NIS, gives an overview of the situation in Germany, provides reasons for its performance and proposes next steps for policymakers.

Startups and Their Importance for Radical Innovation

Startups are newly founded companies with a high degree of innovation and significant growth potential. Very often they are active in the area of new digital technologies. The promise of rapid growth in areas of the new economy explains the increased interest of both investors and policymakers in startups.

The former Internet startups Facebook, Uber, Airbnb and Amazon show an exceptional market capitalization, often without possessing their own physical infrastructure. For example, Airbnb offers rooms all over the world without owning hotels and Uber has needed no cars of its own to turn an industry on its head. This ability to exploit the Internet to achieve universal reach without large capital investment, combined with business models which allow those with assets (a car, a spare room, their creative works or their labour) to commercialize them, is leading to significant disruption in many markets of the world.

Startups disrupt existing industries with digital products, services and innovative business models. Facebook uses a 'free model', allowing free use of its services, but gaining its revenue by making the customers' data their product. Facebook creates revenue by offering customers an attractive social network for staying in touch with friends all over the world and by selling the personal data of these customers to the advertising industry. The music sales business model of Spotify, Apple and Google has changed the landscape completely and is now built on 'lock-in' effects. Users pay a subscription fee for unlimited access to an almost universal library of music instead of buying music on an ad hoc basis, as was practised in the music industry for decades. Amazon uses its market power and scale to disrupt competition by selling below cost price.

These and other Internet startups follow Joseph Schumpeter's (1994) principle of creative destruction, which is fuelled by innovation, entrepreneurship and competition:

> The fundamental impulse that sets and keeps the capitalist engine in motion comes from the new consumers' goods, the new methods of production or transportation, the new markets, the new forms of industrial organization that capitalist enterprise creates. (Schumpeter, 1994, pp. 82–83)

Startups and their digital business models change our economy in the long term, disrupting value creation processes, offerings and customer relationships.

We can differentiate between radical and disruptive innovation (Christensen, 2011). From a company's point of view, radical and disruptive innovation bear high risks. Radical innovation focuses on accessing new markets: such offerings are either world first in performance and function or include huge cost reductions. Disruptive innovation goes even further by directly substituting competitive offerings: LPs were replaced by cassette tapes, tapes were replaced by CDs, CDs by iPods, iPods by streaming; land lines have become secondary to mobile phones; and so on. Disruptive innovation often starts in niche markets or by testing products and services with lead users.[2] A good example is the short message service such as WhatsApp, which challenge the established SMS world, or cloud computing services such as Dropbox that enhance usability and sharing of data storage and have lowered access barriers. Incremental innovation in contrast makes smaller, step-wise improvements, i.e. adding new features to existing products or services in order to improve or maintain a competitive market position. Incremental innovation is favoured by large established companies, which use their 'core competencies' to improve products one step at a time and focus on efficiency, utilizing scale, scope and management techniques to deliver reliably within a set budget and timeframe. Whilst very strong in this mode of innovation, particularly in leading-edge high-tech manufacturing, car manufacturing, chemicals and pharmaceuticals, Germany cannot continue to rely solely on incremental innovation.

Schumpeter emphasizes that capitalism is built on a permanent and continuous turnover in economic and productive infrastructure. This perpetual change of the industrial context forces companies to adapt. The example of Sony demonstrates the consequences of ignoring or missing these waves of creative destruction. Between 1980 and 2000 Sony dominated the portable consumer music market with its Walkman for cassettes. By 2007 Apple had already sold 100 million iPods and achieved up to 70 % market share. For too long Sony concentrated only on hardware, whereas Apple recognized the connection between hardware, software and suitable content, and therefore captured the market. Radical and disruptive innovation is mainly driven by new market entrants, exemplified in this case by Apple.

Table 1.1 The difference between radical, incremental and disruptive innovation

Radical innovation	Prepares for future growth and creates new market opportunities
Incremental innovation	Enhances efficiency and increases profits
Disruptive innovation	Substitutes existing products and services

In the digital age, the new market entrants are likely to be startups. Established companies often have their main competencies in incremental innovation, but over time these competencies become 'core rigidities' (Leonard-Barton, 1995), which inhibit creativity and action outside pre-existing patterns (O'Connor, 1998). Given such barriers, radical or disruptive breakthrough innovations mainly originate with innovative startup organizations (Christensen & Rayner, 2013). This is why it is essential for an NIS to support innovative and scalable startups (Table 1.1).

The next section examines the innovation mix in Germany. It continues the argument that in order to stay competitive, an NIS must support different kinds of innovation.

CASE STUDY: THE SITUATION OF ENTREPRENEURSHIP AND INNOVATION IN GERMANY

The German government has initiated multiple programmes to encourage entrepreneurial behaviour, but the rate of new business formation continues to be consistently low. The Global Innovation Index (Cornell University et al., 2015) and the OECD Science, Technology and Industry Scoreboard (OECD, 2015a) indicate Germany performs well in innovation but poorly in entrepreneurship. In particular, Germany translates its innovation capabilities (education, institutions, legal frameworks, etc.) effectively into new products and services. Out of the 141 countries assessed, Germany ranks 12th in innovation efficiency (which measures the relation between innovation input and innovation output) and eighth in innovation output. However, Germany shows weak rankings with regard to entrepreneurship (Cornell University et al., 2015):

- new business grounding (59th),
- ease of starting a business (93rd),
- ease of protecting investors (49th).

Taking into account the importance of entrepreneurship and radical as well as disruptive innovation to national competitiveness, the German government has introduced both structural push and pull policy mechanisms to encourage self-employment. The Hartz IV reforms include reductions in welfare and benefits, whilst introducing incentives for self-employment (e.g. Gründungszuschuss, Einstiegsgeld). Other initiatives provide coaching for founders or startup loans through vehicles such as KFW Bank and the national EXIST scholarship programme (introduced in 2000 to stimulate entrepreneurship in high technology startups). Considering the country's declining competitiveness in the high-tech sector, the German Ministry for Research (BMBF) has established a high-tech strategy, which makes the funding conditions for Small and Medium Enterprises (SMEs) more user friendly (Die Bundesregierung, 2017).

German government programmes are among the most supportive of those measured in the Global Entrepreneurship Monitor report 2015 (ranked sixth of 62 countries worldwide). However, they seem to not have had a commensurate impact on entrepreneurial activities, which have been low for years. What might be the reasons for the low entrepreneurial output and the lack of efficiency of these support programmes?

INCREMENTAL INNOVATION: A PARTICULAR GERMAN STRENGTH

As illustrated, innovation is a particular strength of Germany, especially incremental innovation:

> Germany [...] infuses its existing industries with new ideas and technologies. For example, look at how much of a new BMW is based on innovation in information and communication technologies, and how many of the best German software programmers go to work for Mercedes-Benz. (Breznitz, 2014)

The country performs well in gross expenditure on research and development (R&D), ranking eighth in the Global Innovation Index 2015. Public and private investment in the automotive and technology sector, advanced manufacturing and chemical industry are high. There is a strong network of public institutions that support established companies with recombining and improving their products. The high level of patent application and tech output illustrate Germany's industrial leadership.

However, despite the leading market position of German SMEs worldwide, the average value of exports still increases significantly in relation to enterprise size (OECD, 2013). The strength of incremental innovation and employment in existing industries is not only highly profitable for German firms: it provides an attractive pathway for talented people and thus displaces entrepreneurship as a desirable career.

The Support Infrastructure for Entrepreneurship Varies Considerably

Germany has improved its support infrastructure for entrepreneurship but in comparison with other countries it is still only average. The Global Entrepreneurship Monitor (Global Entrepreneurship Research Association, 2015) expert rankings place Germany 31st out of 62 countries in terms of taxes and bureaucracy, 39th in internal market dynamics, 32nd in physical infrastructure and 26th in R&D transfer. However, in internal market restrictions or entry regulations the country performs well (ranked fifth out of 62) and ranks tenth in commercial and legal infrastructure. The Global Innovation Index 2015 also underscores Germany's supportive political, regulatory and business environment (with the exception of 'ease of starting a business').

The weak performance in entrepreneurship is not completely due to a lack of government support. There is a strong social and commercial focus on safety and security, and a risk-averse culture reduces the incentive to start a new business (Kelley et al., 2015; OECD, 2015b). Furthermore, the German capital market focuses mainly on established business models, such as services and manufacturing, but shies away from newly emerging industries. With the exception of cities such as Berlin, Munich and Hamburg, the lack of entrepreneurial and technical hubs also plays a role.

Startup Finance in Germany

Investor protection in new businesses is quite poor, ranking 49th out of 141 countries (Cornell University et al., 2015). Access to finance is difficult with Germany ranked 20th out of 32 countries (OECD, 2015c) and

23rd out of 62 countries in the Global Entrepreneurship Monitor (2015) respectively. The OECD study 'Entrepreneurship at a Glance' (2015c) shows no significant improvement in venture capital investments comparing numbers of 2009 and 2014.[3] Access to venture capital is crucial for newly created companies to establish and grow their business owing to a high degree of uncertainty around success. Compared to countries such as the USA, Israel, Canada, Sweden, Korea and South Africa, Germany's venture capital investment as a percentage of gross domestic product (GDP) is very low (OECD, 2015c), accounting for only 0.025 % compared with 0.28 % in the USA (OECD, 2015c, p. 103).

Labour Market and Education

Expert ratings (Global Entrepreneurship Research Association, 2015) have identified considerable weaknesses in both school (ranked 40th out of 62 countries) and post-school (49th of 62) education on entrepreneurship. The university system is also underfinanced compared to the growth in student numbers (which have doubled since 1995). Currently the country invests 1.1 % of GDP in tertiary education (HRK, 2017) and private funds play only a minor role in financing higher education. In contrast, the German dual system of vocational training combining classroom instructions with work experience in established companies and institutions is still envied and copied worldwide.

Founders face difficulties in finding well-educated and experienced co-founders and dealing with payroll taxes and high wages. Established companies have a stronger position in the labour market than newly founded startups, offering higher salaries and better job security. The unemployment rate in Germany has been consistently decreasing for decades (Statista, 2017); there are enough jobs for people looking for work. In 'Cost of redundancy dismissal, salary weeks' Germany ranks 98th out of 141 assessed (Cornell University et al., 2015) and long-term employment regulation makes Germany one of the most employee-friendly countries in the world. These measures increase the attractiveness of permanent work as well as the reluctance of employers to hire new staff: in the event of a termination, employees have the right to a court review of the validity of the termination. A termination may be invalidated if a protection applies. Employers must explicitly state their reason for dismissal.

Culture and Climate Discourage Entrepreneurial Behaviour

The OECD's report Entrepreneurship at a Glance (2015c) selects some indicators as proxies for entrepreneurial culture, such as the level of entrepreneurship education at schools and attitudes towards risk, entrepreneurship and entrepreneurial perceptions. Compared with other countries, Germany ranks only average in entrepreneurial perceptions (perceived opportunities, perceived capabilities, fear of failure) and below average in preference for risk. These results are confirmed by the Global Entrepreneurship Monitor (2015). Germany ranks below average in self-perceptions about entrepreneurship (54th out of 60 countries in entrepreneurial intentions). The country is far below average in the skills and know-how to run a business taught at schools (OECD, 2013, p. 83). More than 20 % of people who do not consider becoming an entrepreneur in the next five years cited 'not enough capital' as the main reason, followed by almost 10 % indicating not having 'enough skills' or 'a business idea'. Almost 40 % are afraid of going bankrupt if they were to start a business (OECD, 2013, p. 86). Additionally, Germany ranks only average by percentage of inhabitants who would give an entrepreneur a second chance if she failed in business (OECD, 2013, p. 87). A recent study which interviewed about 3500 students about their career plans shows that 32 % would like to become a civil servant (Spiegel, 2016). Further, young people in Germany are focusing on a balance between family and career. Starting an own company seems to be too risky, especially if other (attractive) options are available.

The German Model: Analysis of Reasons for Low Performance in Entrepreneurship

There have been no significant changes in Germany in recent years of measures of socio-structural and cultural values in respect of entrepreneurship. Germany is strong in adapting innovations to existing industries. As demonstrated, much of its innovation involves infusing existing products and procedures with new knowledge. This leads to a strong focus on incremental innovation but may reduce the country's performance in radical or disruptive innovation. The German government has made great efforts to create structures to support entrepreneurship, but the effects have been minimal and the development of entrepreneurship has been stagnating for years (Table 1.2).

Table 1.2 The German model – analysis of reasons for low performance in entrepreneurship

Factors which perpetuate the status quo of incremental innovation and permanent employment	– Incremental innovation and growth are strong as is evident by the high performance in innovation outputs and innovation efficiency as well as in the prosperous existing industry – R&D networks between public institutions and established companies are strong and pursue incremental innovation over radical innovation or startups – Jobs, certainty and wealth are connected to structures that have made Germany an industrial powerhouse. A deviation from this course is difficult if not irrational – Secure employment and a stable education system, as well as high salaries, steer young people into institutions rather than entrepreneurship
Factors which work against entrepreneurship	– Low entrepreneurial finance – Labour market and employment inhibitors – Weak entrepreneurial culture, i.e. no appetite for risk or low social status of entrepreneurs in society. Status of being employed in a large company is higher as more secure employment and higher salaries are available – Little or no practical education at school, post-school or in higher education

An Illustrative Comparison with the USA

It is instructive to briefly compare performance in Germany and the USA, a country which is not only an entrepreneurial powerhouse, but also one which leads in the creation of industries in the new Internet economy. In total early stage entrepreneurship, the USA ranks third amongst developed economies (Kelley et al., 2015), and seventh in the attractiveness of entrepreneurship as an attractive career choice (Global Entrepreneurship Research Association, 2015). Conversely, rates of necessity-driven entrepreneurship are generally low.

Support Infrastructure

In the USA, the formal structural requirements for innovative business development (education, institutions, infrastructure, etc.) are ranked third in the world, with high sophistication, competitiveness and government online services (Cornell University et al., 2015). However, these are unevenly distributed, both geographically and socially. Income inequality is high, social mobility is low and paths to betterment are difficult for those who begin the journey with disadvantage. So, as in Germany, the presence and accessibility of support infrastructure present a complex and inconsistent picture.

Financing

Access to finance and investment in new ventures is a great strength of the USA. Venture capital volumes are 17 times greater than in the next high investor country (Japan), making the USA the second highest investor in percentage terms. Where the USA invested over $26 billion in 2015, Germany provided $702 million.

Labour Market

In stark contrast to Germany, the USA has a very poor social safety net, few employee protections, no sick pay policies and a legislated non-existent dismissal period. 'Permanent' employment is not as attractive, and even much less risky than the alternative of self-employment: the third option, welfare, is nothing to aspire to. There is a high rate of university enrolment and the leading technical universities of the world are in the USA. These are closely linked to private firms—and funding—and there is a direct pathway from R&D to new business grounding.

Culture

Cultural and social norms in the USA are highly supportive of entrepreneurship and new business grounding (Kelley et al., 2015), tolerant (if not supportive) of risk and failure, and the successful outcomes of founding a new venture—wealth and image—are highly aspirational.

The American Model

Material conditions and the need for self-reliance, employment regulations which reduce the attraction of permanent employment, significant sources of risk-ready financing and an independent, supportive set of culture norms work together in the USA to provide a consistent and powerful platform for entrepreneurialism and opportunity. The presence of strong technology and business-oriented education leads towards that form of entrepreneurship—Internet-based and radical—that is strongly associated with new American ventures.

SUMMARY AND RECOMMENDATIONS FOR POLICYMAKERS

Support for startups in Germany has improved, but the range of economic, social and cultural factors which restrict them are still not being assessed and addressed holistically. In order to break the current static equilibrium, Germany's strengths also need, perhaps paradoxically, to be put under the microscope. The focus on incremental innovation, learned over time and proven by success, plays a role in displacing the pursuit of radical and disruptive innovation. Why should one change something that obviously works well for companies and, at the same time, gives young employees status, security and reward? The answer lies in the medium- to long-term development of the national economy: will Germany be overtaken by countries in which more risks are taken to develop radically new technologies and business models? Support programmes and policies need to consider not only the weaknesses and gaps in support for startups, but also the existing strengths of the German NIS.

A useful policy for Germany in this context might be greater support for the formation of entrepreneurial groups and networks which collectively, through extended socio-cultural interaction, reshape the cultural milieu which surrounds them to resonate with the existing practical policy inducements. This would replicate the influence of strong entrepreneurial behaviour and networks in the USA. Cities such as Berlin, Munich and Hamburg are in the process of establishing strong entrepreneurial ecosystems. These entrepreneurial hubs attract entrepreneurs and investors from all over the world and therefore increase their attractiveness, which in turn attracts further actors. Perhaps this will lead to the development of new norms and attitudes within extended entrepreneurial groups and for potential entrepreneurs, which can at least provide an alternative framing of risk, failure and professional security. Another method may be the use of leadership figures to promote and raise the cultural status of entrepreneurs, reduce the stigma of failure and break down the impact of the static equilibrium of protectionism. Greater government assistance to increase trust, assist failed entrepreneurs and reduce personal risk may also be helpful.

In conclusion, it is important to be aware of the interactions between culture, social structures and material infrastructures. Without knowing about these dynamics, policy interventions will continue to be a shot in the dark.

NOTES

1. 'National Innovation System means a core concept for analyzing an economy's capacity to produce, commercialize, import, and utilize knowledge and technology. Innovation, learning and technological development, indispensable for long-term economic development of a nation, are now seen as systemic activities involving many and diverse economic actors' (INSME, 2017, para. 1).
2. Leading buyers are early adopters of new methods, technology, services or products.
3. Venture capital is a subset of private equity and refers to equity investments made to support the pre-launch, launch and early stage development phases of a business (OECD, 2015c).

REFERENCES

Ahuja, G., & Lampert, C. M. (2001). Entrepreneurship in the large corporation: A longitudinal study of how established firms create breakthrough inventions. *Strategic Management Journal, 22*(6–7), 521–543.

Audretsch, D. B., Dohse, D., & Niebuhr, A. (2009). *Cultural diversity and entrepreneurship: A regional analysis for Germany.* Paper presented at 24th Annual Congress of the European Economic Association, Barcelona, Spain.

Breznitz, D. (2014). Why Germany dominates the US in innovation. *Harvard Business Review Blog.* https://hbr.org/2014/05/why-germany-dominates-the-us-in-innovation/

Christensen, C., & Rayner, M. (2013). *The innovator's solution: Creating and sustaining successful growth.* Boston: Harvard Business Review.

Christensen, C. M. (2011). *The innovator's dilemma. Warum etablierte Unternehmen den Wettbewerb um bahnbrechende Innovationen verlieren.* München, Bavaria: Vahlen.

Cornell University, INSEAD, & WIPO. (2015). *The global innovation index 2015: Effective innovation policies for development.* Ithaca, NY/Geneva, Switzerland: World Intellectual Property Organization.

Die Bundesregierung. (2017). *The new High-Tech Strategy. The new High-Tech Strategy – Understanding what belongs together.* Retrieved from https://www.hightech-strategie.de/de/The-new-High-Tech-Strategy-390.php

Global Entrepreneurship Research Association. (2015). *Adult population survey measures, 2015.* London: Global Entrepreneurship Monitor.

HRK. (2017). *Higher education finance.* Retrieved from https://www.hrk.de/activities/higher-education-finance/

IBB. (2017/2018). *Förderfibel 2017/2018. Der Ratgeber für Unternehmen und Existenzgründungen.* Retrieved from https://www.ibb.de/media/dokumente/publikationen/wirtschaft-in-berlin/foerderfibel/foerderfibel_2017-2018.pdf

INSME. (2017). *Glossary.* National Innovation System (NIS). Retrieved from http://www.insme.org/glossary/national-innovation-system-nis

Jackson, P., Dobson, P., & Richter, N. (2017). The situational logic of entrepreneurship: A realist approach to national policy. *Innovation: The European Journal of Social Science Research,* 1–24. https://doi.org/10.1080/13511610.2017.1348932.

Jackson, P., Runde, J., Dobson, P., & Richter, N. (2015). Identifying mechanisms influencing the emergence and success of innovation within national economies: A realist approach. *Policy Sciences,* 1–26.

Kelley, D. J., Singer, S., & Herrington, M. (2015). *Global Entrepreneurship Monitor 2015/16 global report,* Babson College, Baruch College, MA.

Leonard-Barton, D. (1995). *Wellsprings of knowledge: Building and maintaining the sources of innovation.* Boston: Harvard Business School Press.

O'Connor, G. C. (1998). Market learning and radical innovation: A cross case comparison of eight radical innovation projects. *Journal of Product Innovation Management, 15*(2), 151–166.

OECD. (2013). *Entrepreneurship at a Glance.* Paris: OECD Publishing.

OECD. (2015a). *OECD science, technology and industry scoreboard.* Paris: OECD Publishing.

OECD. (2015b). Culture: Entrepreneurial perceptions and attitudes. In *Entrepreneurship at a Glance 2015.* Paris: OECD Publishing.

OECD. (2015c). *Entrepreneurship at a Glance.* Paris: OECD Publishing.

Schumpeter, J. A. (1994). *Capitalism, socialism and democracy* (pp. 82–83). London: Routledge.

Spiegel. (2016). *Umfrage. Jeder dritte Student will Beamter werden.* Retrieved from http://www.spiegel.de/karriere/jeder-dritte-student-will-beamter-werden-a-1109900.html

Statista. (2017). Arbeitslosenquote in Deutschland von September 2016 bis September 2017. Retrieved from https://de.statista.com/statistik/daten/studie/1239/umfrage/aktuelle-arbeitslosenquote-in-deutschland-monatsdurchschnittswerte/

CHAPTER 2

What Drives Internet Startups in Berlin? A Qualitative Analysis of the Facilitating and Inhibiting Factors

Nancy Richter, Lucie Volquartz, Thomas Schildhauer, and Konstanze Neumann

Abstract What are the factors that facilitate or inhibit the development of early-stage Internet-enabled startups in Berlin, and how do these factors impact on their decision-making? This chapter gives insight into the local requirements and processes of Internet-based startups. It aims at supporting policymakers to facilitate entrepreneurial processes in Berlin, a city that has grown from a local player into a global entrepreneurial hub.

Keywords Internet startups • Entrepreneurial hub • Berlin • Facilitating and enabling factors • Success factors

N. Richter (✉) • T. Schildhauer • K. Neumann
Alexander von Humboldt Institute for Internet and Society, Berlin, Germany

L. Volquartz
Axel Springer SE, Berlin, Germany

© The Author(s) 2018   15
N. Richter et al. (eds.), *Entrepreneurial Innovation and Leadership*,
https://doi.org/10.1007/978-3-319-71737-1_2

BERLIN: A HUB FOR INTERNET-ENABLED STARTUPS

Following decades of low economic performance, startups in the digital, creative and media industries have been an integral part of the recent boom to Berlin's economy (Richter & Schildhauer, 2016). Building on this base, the city has the potential to become a model for new entrepreneurial activity in Germany. It is therefore crucial to understand the barriers and facilitators for the success of Internet and technology startups in Berlin.

Berlin has developed from a local entrepreneurial hub into a global player. According to the Global Startup Ecosystem Report (2015), up to 3000 tech startups call Berlin home, and have the potential to create up to 40,000 new jobs by 2020. They are predominantly active in e-commerce, gaming and e-marketplaces, and, more recently, as providers of software as a service (SaaS) and ad-tech. However, classical industries such as health, banking and insurance are also being digitized by new startups in Berlin.

In order to identify the main facilitating and inhibiting factors for Internet and tech startups in Berlin we assessed 112 startups. These startups categorized their activities as e-commerce, online marketplaces, SaaS, gaming, media and creative industries, mobile applications, education technology or software engineering. We conducted Startup Clinics (see also Chaps. 3, 4, 5, 6 and 7), during which experts asked founders to review their startup activities and to determine the main factors that either fostered or hindered their development. The founders were given between 30 and 60 minutes to complete the self-assessments, allowing them to thoroughly assess and evaluate their development. In addition, the startups were assessed externally by Startup Clinic experts, increasing the validity of the founders' self-assessment.

The 112 external assessments by the Startup Clinic experts were conducted through a standardized process which allowed qualitative content analysis to be applied and the factors hindering and fostering the development of startups to be explored in a structured manner.

SUCCESS FACTORS AND ECOSYSTEMS FOR HIGH-TECH AND DIGITAL ENTREPRENEURSHIP: THE CURRENT STATE OF RESEARCH

Before presenting the results of the Startup Clinic interviews, this review examines the current state of research into the success factors for Internet and tech startups (see also Appendix).

Based on the three databases Science Direct, Ebsco and Jstore, we identified 175 papers published between 2000 and 2015 on the subject of success factors and ecosystems for high-tech and digital entrepreneurship. The literature review shows different results for different regions, for example Israel, Scotland, Boston (Chorev & Anderson, 2006; Collinson, 2000; van Stijn & van Rijnsoever, 2014). Generally, it can be said that contextual factors are less important than internal factors such as marketing. Particular personal characteristics of founders and the core team such as expertise, commitment, entrepreneurial orientation and qualification, internal locus of control, risk-taking propensity, proactiveness, size and complementarity of team, tolerance for ambiguity, self-efficacy, personal experience and background, working and industry experience are identified as critical (e.g. Block, Brockmann, Klandt, & Kohn, 2008; Jain & Ali, 2013). Clearly, human factors such as attitudes, skills and behaviour are critical to the success of an Internet or tech startup. In the scholarly discourse, there is a consensus that one of the key factors for the successful development of a startup are the skills, attitudes and competencies more specifically of its founders (e.g. Chandler & Hanks, 1994).

FACILITATORS AND INHIBITORS FOR BERLIN INTERNET-ENABLED STARTUPS

Between 2013 and 2015, the Startup Clinic team conducted qualitative interviews with 112 startups during which factors facilitating and inhibiting the development of their success were explicitly discussed. Startups were asked to explicitly raise such factors during the interview. Additionally, the Startup Clinic experts recorded factors not explicitly mentioned but observed by the interviewers. Therefore the factors can be understood as the most significant to the participating startups. Content analysis identified 371 mentions of influences, which were categorized into 38 factors. Twenty-four were mentioned five times or more. The 12 most mentioned factors are discussed below (Table 2.1).

Make or Break: The Critical Success Factors

Critical success factors are those which will make or break an Internet startup business. The factors identified in the interviews were characterized on the basis of whether they exclusively enabled or inhibited success.

Table 2.1   Relevant factors based on the Startup Clinic evaluation

Factor	Characteristics	Mentions[a]	Share of startups[b] (%)
Core team	The entrepreneurial spirit and commitment of the team members	29	25.9
	Complementary skill sets of team members across business and technology	28	25.0
	The network of relationships to external parties for advice and guidance, resources and direction	10	8.9
Team skills	Knowledge of business development and business management	7	6.3
	Experience in entrepreneurship and new business startups	17	15.2
	Knowledge of the specific market or industry context	28	25.0
	Ability and background in marketing and sales	8	7.1
	Technology skills and background	11	9.8
Direct external support		23	20.5
General environment/ecosystem		5	4.5
Finance		18	16.1
Setup of business model	Clarity and definition of the business model	21	18.8
	Quality of the unique selling proposition (USP)	6	5.4
Potential of growth	Market potential of the idea	16	14.3
	Proof of concept of the idea	15	13.4
Product	The costs of product development and launch	8	7.1
	The degree of newness and innovation in the product	10	8.9
	The ability to scale up the business quickly	6	5.4
Marketing	Cooperation with one or more marketing and sales partners	16	14.3
	Having a clear and accurate definition of the product target group(s)	5	4.5
	How much explanation is needed to market or convince potential customers or partners	9	8.0
Law & regulations	Formal registration of the startup as a business company	5	4.5

(*continued*)

Table 2.1   (continued)

Factor	Characteristics	Mentions[a]	Share of startups[b] (%)
	Legal issues surrounding the company and the product	25	22.3
Internal setup/ processes		7	6.3

[a]Factors with fewer than five mentions are not shown
[b]Based on 112 startup interviews which addressed fostering/hindering factors

Some factors were mentioned as equally enabling and hindering. Owing to their prominence in the interviews and their potential to decisively impact the success of startups either positively or negatively, they qualify as critical success factors (Boynton and Zmud, 1984). As critical success factors are vital to a startup's current operative activities, for strategic direction and future success they require continuous and full attention by research.

The five critical success factors for Internet and tech startups in Berlin are:

• the entrepreneurial spirit and commitment of the core team members,
• complementary skills of the core team,
• technology skills and background,
• entrepreneurial experience within the team,
• marketing cooperation with partners.

Three of the five factors identified as 'very important' are properties which are linked to the individuals within a startup: the motivation of the team, their experience in entrepreneurial activity and their complementary skills. It is hardly surprising that the technical resources were rated as absolutely critical by Internet startups and Startup Clinic experts.

The only process-related factor we identified was marketing cooperation; that is, cooperation with established companies and corporations (B2B) or popular consumer platforms (B2C) for marketing and sales purposes. This process supports the rapid growth required by startups in their early stages. Marketing co-operation generates the initial sales channels for an Internet startup and creates visibility in the target market. However, Germany is a country in which cultural norms drive risk-averse behaviour, and this influences the degree to which firms are willing to market collaboratively with unproven startups. Because few firms and public agencies are willing to buy products directly from startups, startups are highly dependent on established partners for their sales pipeline.

Setting the Scene: Inhibiting Factors

Some factors were frequently mentioned by the interviewed startups as being almost exclusively inhibitors to success. These require careful management when establishing a startup. The three most frequently mentioned inhibitors are:

- legal issues surrounding the company and the product,
- clarity and definition of the business model,
- access to finance.

A range of legal issues were raised as constraining and problematic: data privacy regulations and intellectual property, for example (see also Chap. 4). Certain industry types threw up specific legal problems in the area of the business model—for example, the sector of digital health. Most startups mentioned the topic of finance and funding in their interviews, with the issue being one of inadequate access to finance. Only in three cases was securing funding seen as a facilitating factor. Once these constraints are lifted, startups are able to focus on business development and growth (see also Chap. 6). Therefore, a clear and stable framework of laws and regulations around these issues (and access to legal resources), as well as access to funding sources, can be seen as preconditions for fostering startups.

The inability of startups to define their business model and demonstrate revenue streams was also mentioned often by startups and experts as a barrier to success. As this is a crucial part of creating a successful growth strategy, it would seem that education and support in business model development could be a way of providing real assistance to startups (see also Chap. 7).

Make a Business Fly: Facilitating Factors

The interviews identified a number of enabling factors that were identified by the majority of interviewed startups (more than 80 % positive mentions). These can be seen as supporting rapid growth or 'boosting' a business once critical success factors are secured. Two of the factors were linked to the individuals running the startup and their respective skills. Most startups mentioned:

• knowledge of the specific market or industry context within the team,
• direct external support,
• proof of concept of the idea,
• market potential of the idea.

A core, founding team with experience in the target market or respective industry was seen as the most important facilitator and constitutes a substantial asset for any startup. Direct external support, from accelerator programmes, mentors, consultants or institutions such as our Startup Clinics, for example, was also rated highly. In a few cases, such forms of support were also seen as hindering or delaying owing to the associated cost time or decisions that were proven wrong later. For the most part external support was seen as strongly supporting the setup and growth of a business, however. Last but not least, the product and in particular its market potential was seen as a crucial factor to enable entrepreneurial success. According to our interview data, market potential was described by participating startups in many ways; for example, by having found a market niche, or by presenting an entirely new product or technology.

CONCLUSION AND RECOMMENDATIONS FOR POLICYMAKERS

In this research, based on data from 112 interviews with startup teams, we identified 24 factors which had a material impact on success in starting and growing a business. From these we drew out the 12 most important, which we sorted into critical success factors (which must be present) as well as facilitating and inhibiting factors.

What stands out as the most important parameter for success in a startup—in the literature reviewed and in our own empirical research—is the characteristic of a startup team. Research on Israel-based high-tech startups found similar results: the basic idea, the team strategy, the core team's commitment, their expertise and marketing (Chorev & Anderson, 2006). One significant contextual difference is the existence of a highly connected network in the Israeli startup community: in Berlin, these structures are still developing and their absence is strongly felt, which is why it emerged in our data as a key factor (10 mentions).

Policymakers of course cannot intervene and directly influence a founding team, its entrepreneurial motivation or the ideas and respective products. But on a national level, policy can support the creation of an environment that supports and enables startup teams' efforts by considering their needs with regard to legislation, regulations and bureaucracy, and financing.

A recent study (Gründerszene, 2016) highlighted the need to (further) reduce bureaucratic barriers in Germany. Setting up a business takes twice as long in Germany as in the United Kingdom. Tax rates for founders are also higher in Germany and tax return procedures take twice as long. Entrepreneurial education is also an area in which individual competencies of potential founders could be improved. In particular, information technology skills and business development are not part of the basic German curriculum and the technology infrastructure is inadequate in most schools, despite technology education being the foundation for starting up new economy businesses.

At the local and regional level, Berlin's policymakers can foster startup development by attracting financial resources, in particular venture capital. To date, there has been little progress. Furthermore, policymakers should develop local networks and ecosystems: the core team's network, external support and marketing co-operation (especially with large corporations) were identified as important factors enhancing startup success. Existing opportunities for different players to meet should therefore be supported and new ones created. Israel, for example, has built a very dense entrepreneurial network where new founders find expertise and support from established startups and investors. A well-functioning network of founders, educational providers, established companies, investors, customers and regional promotion is key to a thriving entrepreneurial ecosystem. Governments can support these through workshops, mentoring programmes and interactive platforms. They can also consider contracting to startups as their suppliers more frequently, thereby setting an example to other businesses.

APPENDIX

Facilitating and inhibiting factors for software startups—a literature review

Authors	Method	Critical factors	Important factors	Less/least important factors
Chorev and Anderson (2006)	Multi-stage methodology, expert interviews, survey, delphi method	Idea, strategy, core team's commitment, expertise, marketing	Management, customer relationships, research and development (R&D)	Networking, funding type, economy, complete product/ organization *Least important:* general environment and political situation
Song, Podoynitsyna, Van Der Bij, and Halman (2008)	Meta-analysis of 31 empirical studies: identification of 24 most widely researched success factors (Pearson correlations)	Supply chain integration, market scope, firm age, size founding team, financial resources, founders' marketing and industry experience, existence of patent protection		Founders' R&D experience and experience with startups, environmental dynamism and heterogeneity, competition intensity
Kakati (2003)	Identification of 38 criteria: 27 experienced venture capitalists were asked to rate one of their most successful ventures and one of the least successful/failed ventures	Entrepreneur quality, resource-based capability, competitive strategy, ability to develop multiple resource-based capabilities to back up multiple-strategies, ability to meet the unique requirements of customers		

Authors	Method	Critical factors	Important factors	Less/least important factors
Jain and Ali (2013)	Facilitators to entrepreneurial success (all are reviewed in the literature)	Environmental determination; dependency on personal characteristics; 'opportunity recognition sensitivity'; marketing/entrepreneurial/achievement orientation; innovativeness; internal locus of control; risk-taking propensity; proactiveness; reasonable tolerance for ambiguity; self-efficacy; entrepreneurial parents; education and training; work experience; social networking		
Block et al. (2008)	Hindering factors for new business creation in Germany	Difficulties in provision of financial resources, qualified employees, customer relationship/sales, bureaucratic barriers and legal aspects, individual risk tolerance, trust in entrepreneurial competences		
Aspelund, Berg-Utby, and Skjevdal (2005)	Based on longitudinal data from 80 Norwegian and Swedish technology-based startups	Small and heterogeneous teams have an increased probability of survival and overcome counterparts; team competence density; higher degree of technological radicalness increases the probability of survival; early strategic decisions determine the path for new ventures and limit the strategic options at later stages; initial internal resources are antecedents of a technology-based firm's survival		Presence of entrepreneurial experience not have a positive effect on the likelihood of new venture survival
Hyytinen, Pajarinen, and Rouvinen (2015)		Startup's survival probability engaged in innovativeness is lower; interaction of innovativeness and entrepreneurs' higher appetite for risk reduces survival prospects of their startups		Negative association between innovativeness and subsequent firm survival

Authors	Method	Critical factors	Important factors	Less/least important factors
Aaboen, Dubois, and Lind (2013)	Focus on new ventures development, identification of patterns in the network development; method: longitudinal case study of three new ventures, total of 18 interviews; findings: three patterns	Exploration and exploitation of similarities can benefit further relationship development, may impact on ventures' perception of businesses scope; knowledge sharing among customers can be an effective way of expanding the resource base and strengthening the position in the network without developing specific 'user knowledge'; developing relationships with mediating partners expands the customer base and builds a position in the network		
Nowak and Grantham (2000)	Study of the California software industry, main barriers	Lack of access to low cost infrastructure resources, adequate management skills/ knowledge and business networking resources for marketing; prime reason: under-capitalization (lack of experienced management and adequate understanding of seed investing by local investors); lack of a coherent, stable and widely accepted format for structuring early stage deals		
Inderst (2013)		Active investors, such as venture capitalists, can affect the speed at which new ventures grow		
Collinson (2000)	Small indigenous software companies in Scotland, focusing on the strengths and weaknesses of the region's socio-economic infrastructure as a foundation for innovative new business ventures	Two kinds of knowledge particularly important: strategic knowledge (strategic decisionmaking) and knowledge of knowledge (knowledge of finding specific expertise); growth of local clusters of new high-tech businesses linked to local agglomerations of specialist knowledge/expertise; provided knowledge and experience strongly influenced by supporting social, cultural and economic environment of a particular region		

Authors	Method	Critical factors	Important factors	Less/least important factors
Branz and Gleizal (2014)	Investigation on how contextual factors impact the entrepreneur's decision of starting a new business; focusing on Sweden and Brazil; interviews and literature review	Literature review: economic wealth, government policies and procedures, legal and administrative, society's culture, network and knowledge, financial/ non-financial assistance Empirical findings: seven contextual factors do not have the same level of influence in Sweden and Brazil, depend on the environment; most important: network and financial assistance		
van Stijn and van Rijnsoever (2014)	Case study, focus on the role of universities in supporting startups; 42 interviews in the Boston startup ecosystem	Culture of 'paying it forward' and supportive organizations is a fundamental support; balanced and inspirational startup ecosystem; universities and startups naturally have the incentives to sustainably collaborate; universities can promote entrepreneurship as a career path; teaching entrepreneurship demands an 'action-based' approach; ownership, leadership and engagement lead to successful collaboration; universities as excellent piloting sites for new technologies and products		

REFERENCES

Aaboen, L., Dubois, A., & Lind, F. (2013). Strategizing as networking for new ventures. *Industrial Marketing Management, 42*(7), 1033–1041.

Aspelund, A., Berg-Utby, T., & Skjevdal, R. (2005). Initial resources' influence on new venture survival: A longitudinal study of new technology-based firms. *Technovation, 25*(11), 1337–1347.

Block, J., Brockmann, H., Klandt, H., & Kohn, K. (2008). *Start-up barriers in Germany: A review of the empirical literature.* Available at SSRN 1155802.

Boynton, A. C., & Zmud, R. W. (1984). An assessment of critical success factors. *Sloan Management Review, 25*(4), 17–27.

Branz, R., & Gleizal, A. (2014). Entrepreneurship dynamism-The influence of contextual factors on new entries: A comparative study of two business environments: Sweden and Brazil.

Chandler, G. N., & Hanks, S. H. (1994). Market attractiveness, resource-based capabilities, venture strategies, and venture performance. *Journal of Business Venturing, 9*(4), 331–349.

Chorev, S., & Anderson, A. R. (2006). Success in Israeli high-tech start-ups; critical factors and processes. *Technovation, 26*(2), 162–174.

Collinson, S. (2000). Knowledge networks for innovation in small Scottish software firms. *Entrepreneurship & Regional Development, 12*(3), 217–244.

Gründerszene. (2016). *Darum fehlt es den Deutschen an Mut und Ideen.* Retrieved from https://www.gruenderszene.de/allgemein/iw-startups-gruendungen-london-telaviv?ref=nl_b

Hyytinen, A., Pajarinen, M., & Rouvinen, P. (2015). Does innovativeness reduce startup survival rates? *Journal of Business Venturing, 30*(4), 564–581.

Inderst, G. (2013). *Private infrastructure finance and investment in Europe.* Available at SSRN.

Jain, R., & Ali, S. W. (2013). A review of facilitators, barriers and gateways to entrepreneurship: Directions for future research. *South Asian Journal of Management, 20*(3), 122.

Kakati, M. (2003). Success criteria in high-tech new ventures. *Technovation, 23*(5), 447–457.

Nowak, M. J., & Grantham, C. E. (2000). The virtual incubator: Managing human capital in the software industry. *Research Policy, 29*(2), 125–134.

Richter, N., & Schildhauer, T. (2016). *Innovation, Gründungskultur und startups made in Germany.* APuZ. Available at https://www.hiig.de/publication/innovation-gruendungskultur-und-start-ups-made-in-germany-2/

Song, M., Podoynitsyna, K., Van Der Bij, H., & Halman, J. I. (2008). Success factors in new ventures: A meta-analysis. *Journal of Product Innovation Management, 25*(1), 7–27.

van Stijn, N., & van Rijnsoever, F. (2014). *Climate-KIC scout report-the Boston start-up ecosystem.* Utrecht, Netherlands: Universität Utrecht.

CHAPTER 3

Startup Clinics: Applied Research and 'First Aid' for Early Stage Startups

Nancy Richter and Thomas Schildhauer

Abstract The actions and behaviour of early-stage startups are characterized by high levels of uncertainty. It is often the case that the market, the customers and the product are unknown. This is exactly where the Berlin Startup Clinics come into play. With their roots in the English-speaking educational tradition of Legal Clinics, the Startup Clinics provide free support for founders and simultaneously allow doctoral students to gain practical experience. The Startup Clinics in Berlin were extended to include not only legal 'first aid', but also a Finance Clinic, a Business Model Clinic, a Marketing and Sales Clinic and a Human Resource (HR) Clinic. These Startup Clinics support and research early-stage startups as well as offering networks and decision support tools in these phases of great uncertainty for the startup.

Keywords Uncertainty • Early stage startups • Effectuation • Startup clinics • Clinics system • Law clinic • Sales and marketing clinic • Business model clinic • Finance clinic

N. Richter (✉) • T. Schildhauer
Alexander von Humboldt Institute for Internet and Society, Berlin, Germany

© The Author(s) 2018
N. Richter et al. (eds.), *Entrepreneurial Innovation and Leadership*,
https://doi.org/10.1007/978-3-319-71737-1_3

EXPERIMENTING WITH UNCERTAINTY: THE CONTEXT OF EARLY-STAGE STARTUPS

Entrepreneurship is a crucial driver of innovation, economic development and renewal. Within the framework of a national or regional innovation system (OECD, 2013), startups are a source of new ventures, products and services, and they often have high employment multiplier effects (Moretti, 2013). Since entrepreneurship is highly important for an economy, we need a deep and comprehensive understanding of entrepreneurial processes.

Entrepreneurial processes, especially in early-stage business development, are extremely uncertain. When starting to experiment with an idea, startups almost never know what the final product, business model or service will look like. Often their courses of action are diametrically opposed to the settled patterns of more established firms. Peter Drucker put it this way: 'When a new venture does succeed, more often it is in a market other than it was originally intended to serve, with products and services not quite those with which it had set out, bought in large part by customers it did not even think of when it started, and used for a host of purposes besides the ones for which the products were first designed' (Drucker, 1985, p. 189). Schumpeter (2009) argued that economic dynamics and change are caused by innovations, and the economic agent—who introduces innovations and is thus the source of change and creative destruction—is called the entrepreneur.

Since the beginnings of economic thought, entrepreneurship and uncertainty have been mutually interlinked. But as Sarasvathy (2001) notes, scholars, with few exceptions, have generally placed their emphasis on the normative aspects of the phenomenon, rather than on empirical observations of how individuals actually deal with uncertainties in practice. The theory of effectuation instead is grounded in empirical investigations in the field of entrepreneurship (Sarasvathy, 2001, 2008; Sarasvathy & Dew, 2005) and draws upon the distinction between mainstream economic theories, effectual reasoning and the logic of action, which occur in highly uncertain settings.

The theory of effectuation suggests that entrepreneurs do not discover opportunities for new markets only through using reasoned logic and causal analysis. They also create opportunities using alternate logic or 'effectual reasoning'. In the early stages of a new venture effectual reasoning is more successful than causal reasoning (Sarasvathy, 2001). Startups experiment with uncertainty in these early stages by conducting effectuation. While the success of goal orientation and causal reasoning expands as certainty increases, effectuation expands as the degree of uncertainty rises.

What exactly is meant by effectuation and how does it differ from a causal logic of action? In contrast to causal logicians, effectuators start with the means available instead of aggregating means to achieve pre-determined goals. They subsequently co-create or even generate their goals and environment iteratively through commitments with a network of partners, investors, customers and other stakeholders. Effectuation emphasizes alliances and pre-commitments from stakeholders as a way to reduce and/or eliminate uncertainty. Instead of choosing stakeholders on the basis of pre-selected ventures or venture goals, effectuators allow stakeholders who make actual commitments to actively participate in shaping the enterprise (Sarasvathy, 2008, p. 88).

The outcome of an effectuation process depends on the degree to which the stakeholders engage with the process and on what contingencies occur along the way. By acknowledging the open-endedness of the world and seeing multiple possibilities arising in an open-ended situation, effectuators are able to embrace and leverage the unexpected eventualities that arise from uncertain situations, as they are not merely trying to avoid or overcome them, but possibly exploit them.

Early-stage startups need support during the uncertain process of shaping the nascent enterprise. Based upon these assumptions underpinning effectuation, we expect that startups need assistance which resonates with the effectuation process, such as in the following areas:

- shaping an understanding of their own strength and weaknesses,
- expanding their personal network to introduce external creativity and resources,
- support concerning the courses of action,
- interaction with mentors and experts from different fields,
- commitment of relevant stakeholders, such as investors, newly found co-founders, customers and experienced entrepreneurs.

The next two sections present the principles and processes of the Startup Clinics and how we believe they support early-stage startups.

How a 'Clinics-System' Supports Startups in the Early Stages of the Startup Process

Entrepreneurs who are developing ideas to change the world with new products and services frequently encounter a variety of questions especially in the early stages of building a business, when uncertainty is high. Most of these questions concern legal issues, such as business registration, tax issues, employment agreements, trademark and copyright registration, patent application, intellectual property counselling and business modelling. However, there are also other questions relating to business planning and financing.

In the USA, a system of so-called 'Legal Clinics' (sometimes also called Law School Clinics or Practical Law) has been established to support persons in need of legal advice free of charge. Law students in turn gain practical experiences from dealing with these real cases. In Germany and other European countries a similar system has since been developed. For example, student-led initiatives in Passau (Information and Media Law) or Hamburg, (where a Cyber Law Clinic was established to focus on Internet Law in particular). The Cyber Law Clinic has also established a network with the Hamburg Kreativgesellschaft and Mediennetz to support creatives, single founders and teams with Social Media and Internet Law.

Looking at different offerings in the USA and Germany, it seems that there is an increasing trend to provide holistic guidance and support. Therefore networks are established and startups are connected with accounting, business planning and other professionals to provide assistance (Latham & Watkins, 2016). Another trend is to focus on Internet startups, which is also reflected by the European Network of Law Incubators (iLINC), which supports the provision of legal services to information and communication technology (ICT) startups and entrepreneurs.

The processes behind all Legal Clinics are fairly similar. A startup submits an application and is asked to provide basic information about the business. Afterwards, it is invited to a conversation, either a one-on-one session or a meeting with a number of people from various related service providers. Problems are discussed and the meeting ends with suggestions on how to proceed. Sometimes during the session or at a later date, the founder is introduced to an expert or mentor from the Clinic network. This process varies but the aspects of application and subsequent support by a mentor or expert are consistent.

STARTUP CLINICS IN BERLIN

Inspired by the model of Legal Clinics, the entrepreneurship research team at Alexander von Humboldt Institute for Internet and Society (HIIG) offers PhD-led 'Startup Clinics' to discuss challenges with founders of Internet-enabled startups, especially in the early stages while they are experimenting with business ideas. During this process the team also collects data on the startup process. The research goal is to learn more about the status and information needs that startups have in different phases of their development. The Startup Clinics project addresses gaps in research and builds knowledge through the process perspective, which conceives of entrepreneurship as an action-oriented phenomenon.

Entrepreneurship, and especially high growth and innovative ventures such as Internet-enabled startups, are built upon a process of ongoing experimentation (Kerr, Nanda, & Rhodes-Kropf, 2014). Owing to lower startup costs in the software and information technology businesses, the cost of experimentation has declined radically. The frequency of acquiring new information about a product is very high. Internet-enabled startups use information technology to simulate and test their products with customers, and learn whether they will work or not or what customer preferences might be. Through many rapid iterations, startups gain more confidence about their final product or service before going to market. The Startup Clinics at HIIG offer free of charge clinic sessions on the topics of Law, Finance and Controlling, Business Model, Sales and Marketing, and Human Resources (HR). The Startup Clinics focus on Internet-enabled business models and are based upon an holistic approach to business knowledge. The main focus of the Clinic's offering is to learn about interdependencies between questions of law, finance, human resource management and business modelling, and not primarily to consult startups in distinct discipline areas. The advice startups receive is an added value for the entrepreneurs. On the other hand, the overall research goal is to find patterns of enabling and hindering factors for the successful development of startups and reasons for their potential failure.

The Startup Clinic Process

After having registered for a Startup Clinic session, participants receive an invitation to the Startup Clinic's 'meet up' programme for a one-on-one mentoring clinic session with one of the researchers, who is also a startup expert. The doctoral student receives feedback from the startup and the clinic expert to further guide the startup through the uncertain process of founding a company. Finally, after a period of time, the startup is contacted to ascertain how things have progressed. This process is depicted in Fig. 3.1.

There are also specific workshop sessions which support knowledge generation and transfer. Building on the data generated by the clinics and workshops (234 startups and 367 sessions up to 2017), the research group assesses and evaluates the specific challenges founders face, especially in their early stages, and help them overcome difficulties.

When considering the environment and processes of developing a new business under conditions of high uncertainty, it is clear that the Startup Clinic approach is to implement an effectuation logic process. It supports a startup in the early, uncertain stage of setting up a company. It seeks to discover the actual means and resources available, introduces the startup to important stakeholders and engages stakeholder commitment. The Startup Clinics thereby support startups in reducing uncertainty and guide them through a process of iteration, with the goal of increasing confidence in their final product or service before or while going to market. It does this without applying causal or goal-oriented strategic reasoning.

Law Clinic

The Law Clinics are the most sought after in the programme (140 sessions up to 2017). Against the backdrop of high fees that usually arise from external legal services, founders profit in particular from the free services offered by this session. However, while lawyers are paid for answering concrete legal questions and assuming liability for these, the Law Clinic session pursues a more self-help approach, helping startups to help themselves. Its research goal is of course to collect data on the current facilitating and inhibiting factors in the legal domain for Internet-enabled startups. By providing a general screening of the legal issues at stake or an in-depth analysis of the business model's conformity with, for instance, copyright or data protection law (see also Chap. 4), it helps founders evaluate their legal risks. This often results adaptation of their entrepreneurial process and better shaping of their products' value proposition for the market.

For startups, an understanding and awareness of the law is an important enabling factor for coping with the uncertainty they face in their daily business. However, laws do not always fit highly dynamic and mutable

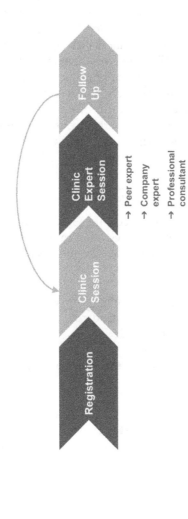

Fig. 3.1 The Startup Clinic process

entrepreneurial processes, which are characterized by the openness of their outcome. For example, the challenge for policymakers is to create legislation which not only protects individuals' fundamental rights but is also open to innovation driven by the (startup) economy while providing legal certainty for both. Focusing on the principle of purpose limitation, the Startup Clinic research examines whether the current legal framework for data protection meets this demand and which alternative legal instruments might be more suitable. Following a multiple case studies approach, the law clinic compares the effects of the principle of purpose limitation currently applied with alternative regulation instruments. With respect to the ongoing legislation process for the European General Data Protection Regulation (GDPR), the Law Clinic organizes several informal workshops with the German Federal Ministry of the Interior, which is negotiating the GDPR on behalf of Germany.

Finance Clinic

The Finance Clinic is the second most popular within the programme. As with other clinics, the bulk of applications come from early-stage startups. Topics that are most relevant to the startups are:

- availability of and access to funding sources,
- business case frameworks and standards,
- structure and layout of pitch decks,
- follow-up and bridge financing,
- performance management (key performance indicator, KPI, systems).

A typical question received from an early-stage startup is simply about where and how to find investors. It is emphasized that the startup needs money to develop a beta version of the product. Other less frequently raised topics include capital management, lead times for venture capital funding and cash flow management.

The research approach in these clinic sessions departs from the dominant 'one-size-fits-all' model used for the early-stage startup financing (see also Chap. 6). Owing to an abundance of software- and web-based ventures, academic research on funding strategies focuses primarily on their specific characteristics. Hardware and physical technology-based startup companies—for example, medical technology, electronics and renewable energy technologies—have fundamentally different requirements for funding sources and funding instruments. The Finance Clinic is concerned with pinpointing these differences and uncovering the explanatory dynamics.

Sales and Marketing Clinic

The focus of the Sales & Marketing Clinics is on the acquisition of customers. They support Internet-enabled startups in approaching the market in the right way and finding an effective sales and marketing strategy for their products or services. Other topics include strategies for finding first customers or identifying the best customer acquisition channels. There are also common questions about one or more of the basic marketing 'Ps' (product, price, promotion and place).

The research is directed towards uncovering the competencies in sales and marketing that are needed to build and grow an Internet-enabled startup and reach profitability (see also Chap. 5). In what combination and degree are these competencies needed?

The most relevant competencies and the ideal level of intensity of each of the identified competencies is being determined through focus groups and expert interviews. Experienced entrepreneurs, consultants and investors within the Startup Clinic mentor network participate as experts in both methods of data collection. The investigation will result in the development of a preliminary competency profile, which will be tested and evaluated through self- and external assessment by founders and Internet-enabled startups participating in HIIG's Startup Clinics project.

HR Clinic

Although recruiting is probably the number one human resource challenge for startups, the HR Clinics also address evaluating competencies to identify a team's strengths and weaknesses. In doing so, they help startups develop an effective HR strategy that includes onboarding, managing, leading, developing and retaining employees. Other key issues include building a company culture as well as managing general challenges caused by rapidly upscaling an organization.

The HR and Culture Clinics are utilized mostly by early-stage startups, and the majority of these are faced with the challenge of finding potential co-founders or their first employees with limited financial resources. In the research literature there is a consensus that one of the key factors for the successful development of a young company is the skills and competencies of its founders and employees. The early employees are especially important for setting the tone and will have nearly as much impact as the co-founders on the future success of a young company (see also Chap. 2). The results of this research will provide guidance for the selection and development of founders and employees in Internet-enabled startups. Critically engaging with one's own and each other's competencies and skills fosters both an awareness of strengths and weaknesses as well as a better understanding of how to exploit the full potential for improvement (see also Chap. 5).

Business Model Clinic

The Startup Business Model Clinics focus especially on early-stage startups. Various clinic sessions have shown that startups particularly want to discuss the elements of their business models, namely products and services, revenue models, customers and their needs, and the value chain, as well as how to pitch their business models to prospective investors. Discussing business model elements often leads to a rethinking of one specific element, but also to a fundamental rethinking of the overarching business model. To allow for this process, we decided to offer business model workshops for startups in addition to the much shorter clinic sessions. The three-hour workshops supplement the one-on-one Business Model Clinic sessions and help startups tackle the aforementioned pain point and create a clearer picture of the particular logic inherent to each startup's business model.

Accompanying Internet-enabled, early-stage startups during the process of finding and adapting their business models has increased our desire to understand the processes underlying a startup's business model development. Until now, research has provided a variety of tools and processes for business model innovation of incumbent firms, but there are few, and limited, attempts to address startup business model development (see also Chap. 7). Our research addresses the entrepreneurial agent's cognition and its effect on the business model development of the startup. Building on that, our research considers initial startup resources and their impact on the business model, and the value proposition creation, more closely. Further, we look at network effects of startup business models. Finally, all previous findings will be synthesized to provide a full understanding of startup business model development. The data to the research are drawn from the minutes of the Business Model Clinics (one-on-one sessions and workshops) as well as follow-up interviews conducted with selected founders.

CONCLUSION

Following the logic of the so-called 'Legal Clinics', the Startup Clinics combine Internet-enabled startup growth and entrepreneurial education. They provide support to Internet-enabled startups, a greater awareness of fostering and hindering factors and the relevance of legal, financial, sales and marketing, HR and business model-related knowledge. The Startup Clinics produce robust business foundations and thereby increase growth and survival rates of young and innovative companies. However, the Startup Clinics also provide a resource base for professional knowledge creation and research to better understand entrepreneurship, its importance to the National Innovation System and also insights into overcoming threats and embracing opportunities deriving from entrepreneurial innovation.

The research conducted within the Startup Clinics has produced several journal articles and conference papers. A summary of this research for each Startup Clinic is presented in Chaps. 4, 5, 6 and 7.

REFERENCES

Drucker, P. (1985). *Innovation and entrepreneurship: Practice and principles.* New York: Harper & Row.

Kerr, W. R., Nanda, R., & Rhodes-Kropf, M. (2014). Entrepreneurship as experimentation. *The Journal of Economic Perspectives, 28*(3), 25–48.

Latham & Watkins. (2016). *Social Entrepreneurship Legal Clinic.* Retrieved from https://www.lw.com/events/social-entrepreneurship-legal-clinic-dc

Moretti, E. (2013). *The new geography of jobs.* New York: Mariner Books.

OECD. (2013). *OECD science, technology and industry scoreboard.* Retrieved from http://www.oecd-ilibrary.org/science-and-technology/oecd-science-technology-and-industry-scoreboard-2013_sti_scoreboard-2013-en

Sarasvathy, S. D. (2001). Causation and effectuation. Towards a theoretical shift from economic inevitability to entrepreneurial contingency. *The Academy of Management Review, 26,* 243–263.

Sarasvathy, S. D. (2008). *Effectuation. Elements of entrepreneurial expertise.* Cheltenham, UK: Edward Elgar.
Sarasvathy, S. D., & Dew, N. (2005). New market creation through transformation. *Journal of Evolutionary Economics, 15,* 533–565.
Schumpeter, J. A. (2009). *Geschichte der ökonomischen Analyse.* Göttingen, Germany: Vandenhoeck & Ruprecht.

CHAPTER 4

Regulation as a Facilitator of Startup Innovation: The Purpose Limitation Principle and Data Privacy

Max von Grafenstein

Abstract Personal data are permitted to be used only for the purpose for which they were originally gathered. This is the basis of the 'purpose limitation principle', which, as one of the key pillars of German data protection legislation, is often hotly debated. The use of this principle is a challenge, not only for startups but also for individuals affected by the processing of their personal data. Where startups often do not know how data may finally be used, and therefore find it difficult to specify precisely or broadly enough the purposes to which a user's data might be put, affected individuals often find themselves in a labyrinth of possible purposes to which their data might be put followed by an endless series of data protection conditions. Users often emerge none the wiser regarding the possible purposes to which their data might be put. Therefore this chapter discusses how the purpose limitation principle might best be applied. The proposal given here allows a non-restrictive, indeed innovation-friendly, application of the principle.

M. von Grafenstein (✉)
Alexander von Humboldt Institute for Internet and Society, Berlin, Germany

© The Author(s) 2018
N. Richter et al. (eds.), *Entrepreneurial Innovation and Leadership*,
https://doi.org/10.1007/978-3-319-71737-1_4

Keywords Purpose limitation • Legal certainty • Data protection model • Standards • Certificates • Purpose standardisation

THE PURPOSE LIMITATION PRINCIPLE: BETWEEN INNOVATION AND LEGAL CERTAINTY

Data protection legislation in general and the purpose limitation principle in particular exist to protect those affected from threats which they cannot anticipate. Such threats can emanate from use of their data by internet start-ups, whose business models are often based upon the processing of personal data. For example, users of social media usually assume that the startup which operates the network uses the data collected to drive its services and the personalisation of advertising. However, they might be surprised to discover that this, or another startup, uses the data to calculate their credit-worthiness—and shares this result with lending institutions, who subsequently approve or disapprove credit or the interest rate to be applied. The purpose limitation principle is intended to protect people from these kinds of unforeseen applications of personal data—and herein lies the problem. Startups have a limited ability to anticipate future uses of data. The strict application of the principle limits the degree to which new content, products, services and business models can be developed. This is particularly the case for Internet-based innovations: development processes are not linear and strategically planned: they are dynamic, emergent and often spontaneous. The results of innovation processes are typically open ended.

This chapter uses results from the Alexander von Humboldt Institute Research Group 'Startup Clinics' (Alexander von Humboldt Institute for Internet and Society, n.d.), which conducted a Law Clinic for startups over a four-year period (see also Chaps. 2 and 3). Four other Clinics were also offered to startups to assist them in their startup endeavours. The Law Clinic analysed the business models of over 100 client startups from a legal perspective, including the effect of the purpose limitation principle on their innovation processes. In the course of this research, it became clear that discussions surrounding data privacy and the purpose limitation principle are characterised by a significant lack of precision. Three key points were consistently overlooked during discussions about the principle, hindering progress towards resolving the tensions between innovation and legal certainty.

One significant building block required to resolve the tension is the creation of data protection legal standards, which are allowed for in the European General Data Protection Regulation (GDPR) in the form of certificates and behavioural guidelines. Using such standards, those organisations responsible for data protection legislation can work with data protection agencies to clarify the legal requirements. This leads to best-of-breed solutions for particular industries (such as insurance) or certain products and service categories (such as e-health apps). Lawmakers are simply not in a position to acquire and apply sector or product specific regulations with the speed required by the highly dynamic and innovative Internet economy.

Therefore, instead of regulating every conceivable area in detail, lawmakers can express their decisions regarding values and acceptability in the form of legal concepts and principles, whose formulation allows scope for self-regulation. In this case, data processing organisations can work with data protection agencies to generate the required industry, product and service knowledge. This process will generally be far quicker and more efficient than the formal law-making procedures. This will require collaborative preparatory work before the actual creation of standards. This aims to create objective measures which can be used to formulate and concretise the purpose limitation principle.

Intended Purpose and the Purpose Agreement in Data Processing

It is noticeable that in debates around data protection and the purpose limitation principle the individual components of the principle are not clearly stated. The first component is the requirement to explicitly state the purpose. This provides the foundation for the second component, that the data may only be used for the purpose that was originally stated and agreed to. Furthermore, the various constitutional protection concepts which determine the functions of these two components are not drawn out. The European Charter of Fundamental Rights contains an independent protection concept which differs from the German right to information self-determination. It is often overlooked that Article 8 Paragraph 2 of the Charter does not state any purpose limitation or earmarking, but only states that a purpose should be specified. The determination of the data's purpose by the data processing organisation is necessary in order to answer the question whether further legal demands should be made of the data processing. One such additional demand can be that of the purpose appropriation. But the constitution does not demand this, at least not according to the Article 8 of the Charter; and the GDPR does not articulate any strict purpose appropriation. The provision only really demands that the processing of personal data should not be inconsistent with the original purpose. Whether this is so can only be resolved by examining each specific case. The concept of protection in Articles 7 and 8 of the Charter has a significant influence on the application of any such case-by-case examination. Clearly, a precise definition of the concept of 'protection' can provide important criteria to startups and help them to reliably assess the application of the data purpose limitation principle for their specific case.

MISSING MEASURES FOR PURPOSE LIMITATION

This leads to the second significant, and often neglected, aspect of purpose limitation. Before the question of consistency between purpose and actual data processing becomes relevant, the question of the precision of the formulation of the purposes of the data collection must be addressed. The more broadly the purposes have been formulated, the less need there will be for these to be changed to allow for subsequent unanticipated data processing. If, for example, the original purpose of the data is that it be used for marketing purposes, then there is no need to reconsider subsequent processing which is directed towards marketing—irrespective of the specific type or aspect of marketing. The GDPR does not address the specification of the purpose and leaves this up to each individual case examination. Unfortunately, this provision provides no criteria for specifying the purpose of the data collection. In the same way, as argued previously, a clear constitutional data protection concept could provide important guidance. The absence of such criteria leads to a high level of legal uncertainty for (internet) startups, who are responsible for data protection and also for those whose data are to be protected. As long as it is not clarified, how precisely these data are to be used, neither the data processing organisation nor the affected users can establish whether the use is permitted or not. Article 29 on Data Protection takes a position on the use of the principle of purpose limitation, but on closer inspection it provides hardly any reliable criteria. The main criterion contained here is purpose consistency (not purpose limitation): the context of the data processing, the kind of data involved, the gap between the new and the old purpose, the possible consequences for the affected party and the protection measures are to be considered. But the Article does not describe how a context is to be defined, how the 'kind of data' is to be classified, how the gap between purposes is to be measured, how to determine the consequences or how protection measures are to be selected or activated.

THE RIGHT TO PERSONAL PRIVACY, LIBERTY AND EQUALITY AS STANDARDS FOR DATA PROTECTION MECHANISMS

In order to address the legal uncertainty, a first step might be to apply all fundamental rights of the Charter, rather than try to limit the analysis to a general basic right to information privacy as described in Articles 8 and 7. The progressive digitalisation of society threatens to render other fundamental rights less important than those about data protection described in these two Articles. This was clearly visible in the so-called Google Judgement. Google was forced to delete the link between the name of a person and the occurrence of their name in an (otherwise legitimate) article about them. The German Constitutional Court has until now examined such questions from the perspective of public self-presentation and freedom of opinion. In contrast, the European Court has focused on data privacy and protection laws, in most cases giving these priority over competing basic rights. In such cases, the court refers to the purpose of the initial publication of an article and the subsequent purpose of the linking of terms via a search engine—without any further specification of what these activities entail.

Such an unclear conceptualisation of this state of affairs has substantial consequences. In the future, the more social behaviour and opinions are developed on the basis of information generated through automation, the more legal conflicts will be carried out under the banner of 'data protection rights' rather than on the basis of other rights. As such, it will become increasingly difficult to tease apart and assess how these other rights are being affected. As long as debate is only carried out in the terms of data protection, the question will immediately be referred back to itself. In contrast, the totality of fundamental rights—the right to personal privacy, liberty and equality—could provide a more refined set of measures to

DATA PROTECTION

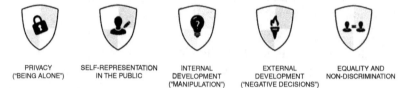

| PRIVACY
("BEING ALONE") | SELF-REPRESENTATION
IN THE PUBLIC | INTERNAL
DEVELOPMENT
("MANIPULATION") | EXTERNAL
DEVELOPMENT
("NEGATIVE DECISIONS") | EQUALITY AND
NON-DISCRIMINATION |

Fig. 4.1   The data protection model

determine the legal position of data processing and the precision required of the data purposes.

If one uses the various guarantees of fundamental rights as presented in Fig. 4.1, it becomes possible to measure the danger of manipulation of individuals through targeted marketing, including its effect on their fundamental right to individual autonomy: one can assess the threat of monitoring and invasive data collection of employees using the concept of professional freedom and use scoring processes against the set of fundamental rights. The purpose limitation principle achieves a new level of functionality by expanding its interpretation to the danger posed by transgression of this principle to various basic rights. The purpose can be articulated broadly or narrowly depending upon the threat posed to those fundament rights.

STANDARDISATION OF DATA USE PURPOSES: A PREREQUISITE FOR DESIGNING PRIVACY BY DESIGN

The question of the precision of the stated purposes to which data can be put, as well as the reconciliation of purposes to actual use, can be resolved by the use of objective measures. How can this be put into practice? Even if objective measures were to exist, in order to do this reliably every data processing step would have to be assessed. The startup engaged in data processing must ask, for every data processing step, whether this is a new purpose and is therefore not allowable. Have we established this clearly and is it consistent with the original purpose? This examination involves significant effort and expense—resources which are usually not available to startups.

The next step in resolving this issue would be the standardisation of typical and routine data processing steps. Data processing organisations should work together with data protection authorities in Standards Committees, which can react quickly and flexibly to the new challenges by formalising and publishing different types of purposes for different contexts. Both users of Internet services and data processing companies could rely on the legitimacy of these data purpose standards. This would encourage innovation and speed without endangering legal certainty.

This idea became more and more convincing during the daily practice of the Startup Law Clinic (see also Chap. 3). In sessions with startups, the various purposes of data processing were discussed. Only in a very few cases was a clear and final legal opinion possible, regarding the formulation of the purpose of the startup's data collection. Even when a startup used external lawyers to suggest formulations and approved these formulations for use, the users were rarely helped, and complained of lack of clarity and confusion. This impression has been confirmed in a number of studies. For example, the Ofcom paper' 'Personal Data and Privacy' looked specifically at the role of the informed consent. They found '*that the consumer seldom reads the conditions of use and if they do, they generally have difficulties in understanding them. It is difficult or even impossible for any consumer to understand the consequences relating to the use of their personal data*' (Wissenschaftliches Institut für Infrastruktur und Kommunikationsdienste, n.d.). With this in mind, a standardisation of purposes for data use may provide an important building block for a practicable and meaningful consent.

ADVANTAGES OF STANDARDS: THE CASE OF CERTIFICATES

It is of course easy to cast doubt on the extent to which such purpose limitation standards can be implemented and how enthusiastically they will be taken up. It is important to emphasise, though, that purpose limitation standards would not be universal: not all instances of data processing would need to adopt standardised purposes, only those that wish to.

There are many advantages to the standards approach. Most importantly, such purpose limitation standards would serve to minimise the legal uncertainty which arises in the current case-by-case examination. Startups would only have to verify that the data processing they envisage falls under a certain standard: this standard would be communicated to the affected party or user. Under these circumstances, the startup can use the data according to this standardised purpose in all subsequent data processing phases. The use of standardised purposes would make it clear to the affected parties how their data might be used. The same effect would apply to changes in purpose. In fact, the GDPR anticipates such privileged use, at least for standards which take the form of certificates. At the very least, the data protection requirements contained in a certificate give a level of confidence that subsequent data processing applied to a person's data will comply with the law and regulations.

The use of certificates can also ensure that data transfer to third parties or other countries is still supported by a legitimated legal framework. This is of great interest for data exchange with the United States and the United Kingdom. In the USA, the future of the so-called 'Privacy Shield' is uncertain, owing to recent legal and political developments. The exit of the UK from the European Union will reduce the country's status to that of a third party. Data transfer to such countries could be legitimated through the use of certificates, as these can be anchored in appropriate control and sanction mechanisms. Organisations outside the European Union can gain access to personal data from the inner European market if they adhere to the control and sanction mechanisms of standards, for example in the form of certificates.

Open Questions for Purpose Standardisation

In the final analysis, standards have the advantage of being more efficient and streamlined than lawmaking. Standards bodies can react more quickly to technological, economic and social developments; and, as is appropriate, the GDPR allows that the certification processes consider the needs of small and medium-sized enterprises. In contrast to this, cumbersome lawmaking processes often produce laws which are outdated by the time they are implemented. Legal standards for data use purposes can provide a balance between innovation and legal certainty—and therefore create an important foundation for a well-functioning data ecosystem. Of course many questions remain open. The most important of these is whether the GDPR allows the standardisation of data processing purposes. A strong argument in favour of this is that the appropriate prescriptions relate to specific data processing tasks, and these tasks cannot even be considered for initiation by an organisation without a statement of purpose. The standardisation of the data processing steps would contain the processing purpose. A further open question is how detailed and precise such standardisation will need to be in order to achieve the required level of legitimacy and trust—especially in the minds of those affected. Finally, and in reality, it is not clear whether powerful Internet companies will accept such standards or prefer individual case-by-case examination. Nevertheless, as long as standards do not exclude other means of assessment, it is unlikely that they will do any damage.

This chapter provides suggestions for the application of the purpose limitation principle to the practice of data processing organisations as well as the everyday use of systems by consumers. Internet-based startups, which in the course of rapid and radical innovation move in a domain of great uncertainty, may profit the most from suggestions such as these (see also Chap. 1). More work is required to add detail and depth to these ideas, and many questions remain open. The level of detail which is required to describe a particular purpose, or whether a new purpose is consistent with the original one, can only be resolved by consulting with those affected. Only when users understand and trust the data use conditions, and are confident that subsequent misuse of data is excluded, will they use the services and products from which data is to be gathered. The same is true of organisations that purchase data-oriented applications from startups for their own use. The organisations are more likely to purchase them when they can be assured that they are not transgressing data protection laws. Standards, for example in the form of certificates, may provide a useful means of sending clear signals to users and organisations about the consistency of data use with relevant data protection laws.

References

Alexander von Humboldt Institute for Internet and Society. (n.d.). *Innovation und Entrepreneurship*. Retrieved from: https://www.hiig.de/en/project/innovation-and-entrepreneurship/

Wissenschaftliches Institut für Infrastruktur und Kommunikationsdienste. (n.d.). *Personal data and privacy*. Retrieved from: http://www.wik.org/index.php?id=687

CHAPTER 5

Do You Have What It Takes to Become an Internet Entrepreneur? The Key Competencies of Successful Founders

Martin Wrobel

Abstract Marketing and sales competencies are crucial for founders setting up a new business. This chapter investigates what competencies founders need to develop in order to make the marketing and sales activities of an Internet-enabled startup successful and lead it to profitability and growth.

Keywords Marketing • Sales • Competencies • Credibility • Willingness to learn • Customer orientation • Communication skills • Perseverance • Resilience • Analytical capacity • Results orientation

BACKGROUND

Startups are amongst the key drivers of innovation and change within the dynamic contemporary business environment. Successful entrepreneurs can very rapidly disrupt entire sectors and either go on to manage them as growing and influential participants or exit for large sums as they are

M. Wrobel (✉)
Alexander von Humboldt Institute for Internet and Society, Berlin, Germany

© The Author(s) 2018
N. Richter et al. (eds.), *Entrepreneurial Innovation and Leadership*,
https://doi.org/10.1007/978-3-319-71737-1_5

bought out by other firms. In general, the challenges to new business grounding, such as access to finance, technology and business knowledge, have become more manageable as governments and the private sector have sought to smooth the pathway for these new entrepreneurs. And the incentives to create a new business have never been greater than they are today.

Most startups still fail, however. Two dimensions of this failure stand out as recurrent (see also Chap. 2):

- the founders and their competencies,
- the startup's marketing and sales activities.

Since launching in 2013 as a research project, the Startup Clinics programme run by the Alexander von Humboldt Institute for Internet and Society has supported almost 250 founders (see also Chap. 3). Analysis of the data collected through the project has shown that first-time founders in particular are confronted with unknown and unexpected circumstances, and that their existing knowledge and previously gained qualifications are generally not sufficient to successfully overcome the challenges they face.

These new situations are the reason why founders need to equip themselves with competencies that enable them to act appropriately and solve the problems that arise (Erpenbeck & von Rosenstiel, 2007). Competencies are more than just knowledge, skills and qualifications. They are task focused and performance oriented (Erpenbeck, 2010; Heyse & Erpenbeck, 2009). As shown in Fig. 5.1, competencies are generally differentiated into several categories: personal competencies, activity and action competencies, social and communicative competencies, and professional and methodological competencies.

In contrast to personal traits, competencies are generally easier to learn and develop. This suggests, first, that competencies are closely related to the actions they engender, and that secondly, people with weakly developed competencies in important areas have scope to develop them.

According to several studies, the biggest challenges for founders and their startups are customer acquisition, and marketing and sales (Kollmann, Stöckmann, Linstaedt, & Kensbock, 2016; Marmer, Herrmann, & Berman, 2011; Ripsas & Tröger, 2015). Thus the role of the 'Marketer' is central in the development of a startup, be it for a single founder or a

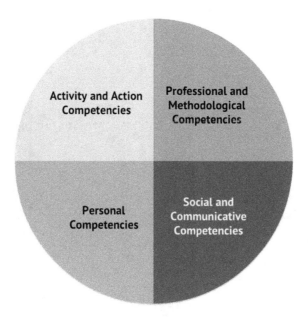

Fig. 5.1 The four competence categories

member of the founding team. Founders should pay particular attention to those part-competencies which are most relevant to the process of setting up a business. The right competencies in the areas of marketing and sales can, after all, decide whether a startup will fail or succeed.

WHAT COMPETENCIES ARE NECESSARY IN MARKETING AND SALES TO ENSURE A STARTUP'S GROWTH?

Expert discussions with more than 15 experienced founders have shown that there are eight central part-competencies (level 1) that the individual in charge of marketing and sales should ideally demonstrate. Based on these is a group of 11 further part-competencies (level 2) which also play an important role depending on the situation and the context. These competencies are shown in Fig. 5.2.

The following sections introduce the eight part-competencies identified at level 1 and illustrate those using citations from expert founders.

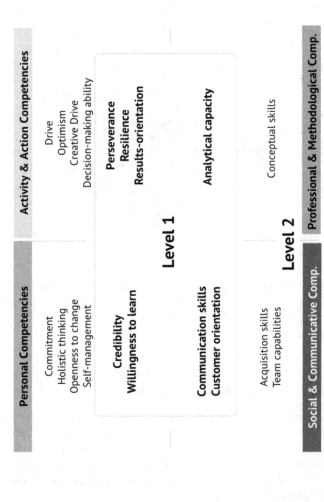

Fig. 5.2 Part-competencies as part of the competencies profile

Credibility

Credibility plays a central role in the relationship startups have with their various stakeholder groups, be they customers, suppliers, first employees, co-founders or potential investors. Acting in an authentic way helps to address the respective groups in the appropriate way and to gain their trust. Startups tend to hold the shorter end of the stick in any negotiation and credibility helps in levelling the playing field.

> You need to convince a lot of people of what you do. And you will only succeed with this if you yourself display credibility. Because, especially in the beginning, people aren't dependent on you. They don't need to work with you. And they will only do it if you are trustworthy.[1] (expert 8)

All marketing and sales activities undertaken by a startup need to convey complete credibility. This does not only apply to direct communications with customers, but also during other sales activities and in the creation of marketing collateral such as online advertisements, pitch decks or social media presence.

Willingness to Learn

A newly founded company is nothing but a collection of unproven assumptions. To take a company forward and achieve the goals set out, founders need to be willing to learn from their conversations with customers, the observation of their reactions and the company's environment, and to abandon existing hypotheses and create new ones. This period therefore coincides with a series of changes to the business model that any innovative startup must contend with.

Willingness to learn is especially important as the requirements that are placed on the founders might change quite drastically. Rapid growth from one to 100 employees can require a transformation in the role of the founder or founding team.

Founders with a strong willingness to learn and adapt therefore have the best chances to develop successfully in tune with their growing company. Finally, a willingness to learn new skills is also crucial in order to fill gaps in a founder's knowledge and quickly to gain a well-grounded understanding of new and complex issues.

> In hindsight, we didn't have a grasp on the situation one little bit. For example, I am no SEO [search engine optimisation] specialist, but I was able to make it work for us. Or similarly with SEM [search engine marketing] campaigns, I knew that they existed and that there were some criteria, but I had no idea how to work that programme. For a while we also didn't have a graphic designer, so I just taught myself how to use this graphics programme one day. It is just unbelievable how many new things come up every day. And everything just needs to go super fast, you need to know what to do, what you want, what the company wants and needs. And in the end, it really doesn't matter if you studied business or law, you just need to deliver, you need to be able to do what someone who studied it would. (expert 10)

Communication Skills

Not every member of a founding team necessarily needs to be a natural at communicating. However, there should be at least one person who excels at it, and he or she should be in charge of both the marketing and sales activities. Furthermore, the ability to communicate clearly and effectively is, similar to credibility, an important ingredient in relationships with the various stakeholder groups (i.e. suppliers, customers, employees, co-founders, investors).

Startups face the challenge of proving their credibility to their stakeholders: they need to build up trust in those relationships. As a new company, initially one has no reputation with the stakeholders, and for them it is not clear if the company will still be operating in three or six months.

> Good communication skills have nothing to do with being talkative and also do not mean that one is constantly communicating. It is more the ability to understand how to communicate, or the ability to communicate in the right way. It means being able to clearly express one's thoughts and to structure conversations and to be able to clearly and concisely get the message across. And listening, too. That's really important.
>
> And that means having a capacity for empathy and the ability to understand what kind of person is sitting across the table from you. And in the next step, to be able to adapt one's style of conversation to them and solve their issue. And to communicate it in a way that in the end characterises that person. (experts 9 and 14)

Good communication skills, however, go further than verbal communications; they also cover non-verbal and written communication. For example, well-structured, targeted and concise emails without spelling mistakes that get the message across to the client are extremely important. The same applies to so-called live chats, which are becoming an ever more popular method of contacting customers directly.

Customer Orientation

To listen to customers, understand their problems and find new, innovative and better solutions than are currently available is the core business of any startup. Being in touch with the customer and receiving feedback on one's products is essential. Especially in the early phases, dealing with the received feedback in a clear and honest way is very important.

Customer orientation is important for both marketing and sales activities and starts with planning. For founders, it is important to see any issue through the customer's eyes and to be able to switch perspectives in order to understand what the customer is really thinking. All activities and the behaviour of the startup should be adapted accordingly.

To verify reality as perceived by the customer, founders need to take a step back and rein in their own notions and assumptions.

Customer orientation is incredibly important and really number one for new business acquisition. The most successful businesses truly put the customer at the centre of their work. As a startup, if one can't understand what the customer wants and can't react to changes in customer or market behaviour, one will be out of the market in no time.

In the end, it's the customers who decide what they want and what not and we all need to play by their rules. (experts 8 and 14)

Customer orientation is generally addressed as part of sustainable, fair and long-term customer relationships. In order to develop a successful startup, customer relationships need to be understood as a long-term investment. There is thus no benefit in acquiring new clients if the company will not be able to serve them in the long term owing to a misaligned service offering or inappropriate product development.

Perseverance

Perseverance is a crucial factor in overcoming resistance in the initial stages of starting up a business. Resistance might come from customers, investors or other stakeholders if they are not convinced by the idea, the product or the service. Founders need to strongly believe in their mission, and if they react to setbacks with tenacity and resilience they will be able to overcome the difficulties that arise in the early stages of their company.

> Perseverance to me is a crucial meta-skill. Without that skill a person in my eyes is not a good fit for a startup, particularly in a central function during the early stages. I think the worse situations are those where you feel like you have no options. No matter what you do, there is no solution.
>
> Financing can turn into such a perceived dead end. We also had times during which technology was a real nightmare. This happened during the holiday shopping season where you lose the sales of an entire year, where you have no solution and can't decide on what to do. Or all of a sudden your customers go on the warpath. (experts 6 and 10)

Perseverance in marketing and sales is crucial to success. It is also important not to give in to rejection or failure, but instead to stick with it, to understand why it happened and to change things where appropriate. Therefore perseverance and flexibility should be adequately balanced. Founders need to find their own balance between perseverance and believing in their own idea on the one hand and openness and flexibility to change things that don't work on the other.

Resilience

Startups are characterised by a high degree of uncertainty. That uncertainty is often substantial, as it is frequently unclear whether the startup will still exist in a few months' time. Exceptional conditions need to be managed, such as working for months on end before getting some positive reactions from customers or investors or having your back to the wall because the next financing round has not been secured two weeks ahead of the next salary pay date. Such situations can put extreme pressure on founders, both physically and psychologically.

Particularly extreme situations show how resilient founders are. Optimism and resilience—which can be expressed as a tolerance for frustration—are very important characteristics. Setbacks should always be expected, as most things do not go exactly as planned.

> Building a company is incredibly hard work. I worked 18 hour days during the week and ten hour days on the weekend.
> I put up high racks till four o'clock in the morning because nobody else did the job. (experts 12 and 8)

> Once you get people to work for you, in our case a woman in customer service who previously had a permanent fixed contract, you really start to worry while you are still going through a round of financing. You must be able to handle that kind of pressure. You really carry an unbelievable responsibility towards these people. Because if things go wrong, you have to tell the people that you hired only a few months back: 'Sorry, it didn't work out'. And maybe that person just built a house and got a mortgage. You must be able to handle that pressure because on the other hand you have got a responsibility: maybe you have to let that one person go so that three others can keep their job. (expert 8)

Results Orientation

Startups generally need to show results quickly and therefore, particularly in the early stages, a strong focus on the bottom line is decisive. Results orientation as a part-competency is especially relevant to the areas of marketing and sales, as these are the areas where measurable results or turnover are generated.

> Results orientation simply means working without meetings, without drawing up plans, and where internal or external get-togethers don't happen to identify next steps or to say things such as: yeah, hmm we could do it that way. But it should instead go like this: Who is doing that? You do part A and I'll do part B and who is going to do part C? When will this be done by? We will do it by next week. Let's meet middle of next week to clarify where we are at and to answer remaining questions. So there will be a follow-up meeting and a defined goal and clear responsibilities for each person and strict deadlines until when things should be done. That, to me, is results orientation. Nothing is left to chance; everything is divvied up in such a way that each person has clear responsibilities. (expert 15)

Two qualities are important to work in a results-oriented fashion: first, knowing what one's targets are and their place within the bigger picture; and secondly, focusing on what matters and to be able to getting those things done. Results orientation means continuously refocusing all activity on results. For marketing this means defining goals, starting activities, measuring results and consequently analysing what has worked and what has not.

Analytical Capacity

Companies are systems that work according to particular rules. Having the right analytical capacity and judgement helps to better understand those rules and how a company works. Having the right analytical capacity helps in assessing test results of a particular working hypothesis, recognising what has worked and what has not, and deriving actions to improve or optimise.

Especially during the early stages, being able to make decisions in a quickly changing environment, and based on numbers and data, is incredibly important: will this marketing or sales activity deliver the right results for our company?

Marketing activities can take a myriad of forms and functions for any startup. For some business models or marketing channels, analytics might not be that important, for others it might be a critical success factor. Sales also require strong analytical capabilities.

> Startups, in the beginning, often can't afford to hire a specialist and the founder simply has to employ his own capacity to abstract and analyse to the best of his abilities; ensure that one 'thinks big' on sales from the get-go and also stays on top of the operative implementation, ensuring that it is realistic and ultimately achievable. (expert 7)

This also holds true for direct customer interactions. To immediately take in and get to the bottom of the issue at hand, understanding what the client's responses really mean and directly responding to these, founders not only require high empathy levels and good communication skills but must also be able to think on their feet and have sufficient analytic capacity.

An overview of further important part-competencies can be found in Fig. 5.2. Readiness to get things done, big picture thinking, openness to change, good self-management, strong drive, optimism, creativity, ability to make decisions, deal closing skills, team spirit and a strong conceptual understanding are all significant.

Each of these part-competencies should ideally be highly developed, but extremely developed part-competencies can also inhibit good outcomes. An overly optimistic view can quickly turn to simple-mindedness, for example, if the circumstances do not warrant it. Openness to new ideas might tip into arbitrariness and therefore lead the startup astray. Competencies must in this context always be considered to be soft skills, to be applied with balance and good judgement.

The results show that in the initial phase of setting up a company, professional and methodological competencies, that is particular skills or market knowledge, are less relevant than a set of more generic competencies. Personal competencies and activity- and action-based competencies are the most important for the marketing and sales activities of a startup during the early phases of its development.

Next Steps for Startups: How to Develop Competencies

Irrespective of whether lean startup, customer development or design thinking is applied, the part-competencies introduced above are strongly represented in today's most popular entrepreneurship philosophies.

Lean startup refers to the process by which founders take an unfinished prototype to market as quickly as possible (see also Chaps. 8 and 10). The ongoing iterative development is then based on real-time customer feedback. Through this model a business can be successfully set up with little capital and by applying simple, direct processes.

Customer development is a comparable concept which develops innovative products and services through a four-stage process based on real customer problems.[2] At the point of product–market fit this also delivers an ideal base to initiate the related marketing and sales activities.

Finally, the design thinking method focuses on solving problems and developing new ideas by putting the user and client needs front and centre (see also Chaps. 8 and 10).

Customer orientation and willingness to learn new things are two basic components of the above described approaches, and are often the main reasons why startups are able to develop prototypes, acquire customers and develop them into a business model so quickly.

Results orientation is probably one of the biggest differentiators between startups and established businesses. While larger companies more often tend to be more process oriented than results oriented, startups have no choice but to deliver results rapidly. Process orientation is generally manifested in the more rigid adherence to rules, structures and processes that is expected from individuals within larger organisations.

Faced with a high likelihood of failure, founders need perseverance and resilience to overcome the resistance and setbacks that they will inevitably be faced with, and despite which they will succeed nonetheless.

While on this journey, founders are aided by a large analytical capacity which helps them filter, sort and analyse the mass of information they receive and develop the right actions and decisions based on this. They will not succeed in winning over all important stakeholder groups (e.g. customers, suppliers, employees, co-founders and investors) if they have not developed the right communication skills or are not considered to be trustworthy.

There is generally no job description for the role of an entrepreneur, as they exist for employees, managers or leadership roles in small and large businesses. First-time founders should therefore urgently consider what competencies they might need to succeed. Examining one's own competency levels also creates a good awareness of inherent strengths and weaknesses and the resulting personal potential. Being a first-time entrepreneur means doing many things for the first time. Competencies can support founders to face emerging challenges and overcome hitherto unknown situations.

What can and must founders do to acquire the right competencies? Initially, a 360-degree assessment can help to discover if and to what level founders already display the aforementioned competencies and where there are gaps to be filled. If shortcomings are identified, this can be used as a point of departure to develop the needed competencies. The exact makeup of such a plan is highly dependent on the individual part-competencies and their scalability.

Communication skills, customer and results orientation, for example, are easier to develop than resilience and analytical capacity. Generally, all competencies are best developed through trial and error in the real world, and thus failing at a first attempt to set up a business should not be considered a personal failure. If founders are able to take this as an opportunity to learn from mistakes, they are instead more likely to succeed the next time.

NOTES

1. Experts' opinions were recorded as paraphrased quotations.
2. The four stages are customer discovery, customer validation, customer creation and company building.

REFERENCES

Erpenbeck, J. (2010). Kompetenzen: eine begriffliche Klärung. In V. Heyse, J. Erpenbeck, & G. Ortmann (Eds.), *Grundstrukturen Menschlicher Kompetenzen: Praxiserprobte Konzepte und Instrumente* (pp. 13–19). Münster, Germany/New York/München, Germany/Berlin, Germany: Waxmann.

Erpenbeck, J. & von Rosenstiel, L. (Eds.) (2007). *Handbuch Kompetenzmessung: Erkennen, verstehen und bewerten von Kompetenzen in der betrieblichen, pädagogischen und psychologischen Praxis.* 2. Überarbeitete Auflage, Stuttgart, Deutschland: Schäffer. Schäffer-Poeschel, Stuttgart, Germany.

Heyse, V., & Erpenbeck, J. (2009). *Kompetenztraining: 64 Modulare Informations- und Trainingsprogramme für die betriebliche, pädagogische und psychologische Praxis.* 2. Überarbeitete und erweiterte Auflage. Stuttgart, Germany: Schäffer-Poeschel Verlag.

Kollmann, T., Stöckmann, C., Linstaedt, J. & Kensbock, J. (2016). European Startup Monitor. Bundesverband Deutsche Startups e.V. Retrieved from https://goo.gl/b3yJUm

Marmer, M., Herrmann, B. L., & Berman, R. (2011). *Startup Genome Report 01: New framework for understanding why startups succeed.* Retrieved from https://goo.gl/gXOCWW

Ripsas, S., & Tröger, S. (2015). *Deutscher Startup Monitor 2015.* Hochschule für Wirtschaft und Recht Berlin, Berlin, Germany. Retrieved from https://goo.gl/aG4X0l

CHAPTER 6

Startup Financing in Berlin

Robin Tech

Abstract Financing plays an essential part in the success of most startup enterprises. In this chapter, three essential questions of fundraising in Berlin in particular, but also in the wider context, are addressed. First, the kind of funding that an entrepreneur should be seeking is examined. Then the prerequisites and supporting factors of raising capital from investors are explored. Finally, the current status of the Berlin startup financing scene and its outlook are noted.

Keywords Startup funding • SME funding • Venture capital • Business angels • KPIs • Public funding • Social capital • Crowdfunding • Bootstrapping

INTRODUCTION

Berlin, which is currently touted as the centre of German startup activity, has received a substantial amount of media attention over the past three years. The number of startups has grown substantially, there is a constant influx of entrepreneurs, and, more recently, an increasing volume of venture capital funding. A close inspection of funding rounds reveals that

R. Tech (✉)
Alexander von Humboldt Institute for Internet and Society, Berlin, Germany

© The Author(s) 2018   65
N. Richter et al. (eds.), *Entrepreneurial Innovation and Leadership*,
https://doi.org/10.1007/978-3-319-71737-1_6

investment volumes are indeed appreciating in breadth and size. But the numbers are also heavily skewed and volatile. Berlin-based startups received a combined 1.46 billion Euros in startup financing in the first half of 2015, yet this figure halved in the first half of 2016 and came down to 520 million Euros by the end of 2016. Heralded as Europe's new centre of venture capital in 2015, Berlin fell back to fourth place in 2016. London, with 1.3 billion Euros, was in first place, Stockholm (1 billion Euros) second, and Paris (673 million Euros) in third place. The inconsistency in funding levels over time can be explained by particular one-off events, for example very large funding rounds for individual startups. Rocket Internet, the Berlin-based company builder, and the fintech startup Kreditech alone were responsible for about half the investments made in the first half of 2015.

This chapter attempts to shed some light on the financing situation for Berlin-based startups from a practical and grounded perspective, beyond the hype. Data from the German Startup Monitor ("DSM" for Deutscher Startup Monitor), other recent, Berlin-focused publications, and learnings from the Startup Clinics program of the Humboldt Institute for Internet and Society (HIIG) were used. This chapter is explicitly aimed at nascent entrepreneurs who are in the process of starting their venture and have their eye on external capital to finance their endeavor.

Startup Funding Versus SME Funding

To identify the right source(s) of funding for a nascent entrepreneur and her venture, the entrepreneur needs to determine what type of company she wants to build. Thus a distinction between different kinds of newly founded companies seems appropriate. In this chapter I differentiate between startups and young small and medium-sized enterprises (SMEs). The main difference between these lies in their potential to scale and grow very rapidly. Blank (2014) stated that startups are not simply smaller versions of corporations and established companies, because of a startup's absolute focus on scale. This includes scaling revenues, headcount, market share, and other vital aspects of fast growth (OECD, 2014). Startups aspire to grow big very quickly on multiple levels, although this can take up to a decade (Davila, Foster, & Gupta, 2003). Young SMEs, on the other hand, are more traditional, in that their founders seek to build a sustainable business that yields a profit quickly. Their main aim is to create a business that can sustain itself and its founders. This is why many SME founders remain with their company for much longer than startup founders. An attribute that both nascent venture types share is that their business model and/or technological approach needs to be innovative in some way. This allows them to gain market shares and survive.

Why is it important to distinguish between startups and SMEs? Because both types of companies attract different kinds of investors and raise external capital from distinct sources. Startup funding focuses on financing scaling activities; SME funding finances organic growth and sustainability. In the following, the various funding sources for startups are briefly discussed against the backdrop of young venture funding in general.

Where Founders Think Funding Comes From—and Where it Really Comes From

Many founders who participated in the Startup Clinics program expected to eventually raise funds from venture capital (VC) firms. This is understandable. According to a recent study prepared by Pricewaterhouse Coopers (PWC) and the National Venture Capital Association (2015, 2016), the share of early stage VC investment dollars compared with the total startup investment is at historic highs similar to those of 1996. Most of the nascent entrepreneurs will, however, never raise VC or any external capital for that matter. Startup funding can come from various sources. But we need to recognize that—even within the domain of startup funding alone—investment strategies differ greatly between investor classes. Motivations and prerequisites to make an investment vary significantly between business angels (Bas), VC firms, and banks, for example.

The initial source of startup capital is most often the founders and their friends and family. This type of funding is called bootstrapping and FFF financing—which stands for 'friends, family, and fools' (Manolova, Manev, Carter, & Gyoshev, 2006). While much more common in the US, German startups use bootstrapping as well (DSM, 2015).

The second source of funding—and possibly the most important one for startups—is BAs. These investors are wealthy individuals who support unlisted startups with their private money—but they are also the least understood group of investors. In the case of Berlin-based startups and BAs, one can assume that most tend to be unsophisticated investors, unable to add significant value to the firm (Fairchild, 2011, p. 360). This is likely owing to the immaturity of the local startup ecosystem and the inexperience of Berlin-based BAs compared to their US counterparts.

Banks—such as the Sparkasse Berlin or the state-owned IBB—can provide financing by means of short term credit card overdrafts, mortgages, and non-specific and specific loans. However, banks are rather uncommon financiers for startups owing to tight regulations and risk profiles: the chances of success, profit and loss expectations, or business plan aspirations of startups often do not fit into this framework (Schramm & Carstens, 2014).

Public subsidies, on the other hand, are key startup financing sources. Financial contributions that public bodies make to start companies include non-repayable grants—such as the EXIST program in Germany—and subsidies, low-interest loans, and tax exemptions. Berlin, with its rich university and college ecosystem, offers myriad support programs that include rent-free office space, consultancy, and no-strings-attached cash contributions. Other notable capital sources are startup competitions by the Medienboard Berlin-Brandenburg or the Berlin Senate Department for Economics, Energy, and Public Enterprises. Public subsidies in general are an often overlooked but one of the most important sources of SME funding and startup financing in particular (Duhautois, Redor, & Desiage, 2015).

Crowdfunding is becoming a relevant source of startup funding. The different kinds of crowdfunding are reward-, donation-, and equity-based crowdfunding as well as peer-to-peer lending (Schramm & Carstens, 2014). These differentiations are important, as each crowdfunding scheme entails vastly different implications. Media-focused startups might dominantly opt for donation-based crowdfunding, while hardware startups can use reward-based models to pre-sell their product.

VC firms are probably the most prominent and glamorous startup financier. These firms focus on high-risk and high-return opportunities and invest money pooled from external investors—so-called limited partners—who have made an investment in the VC fund. It is vital to understand that these funds always have a defined and limited runtime—often about eight years. During this time, VC managers have to identify startups, screen them, invest for equity stakes, and divest to liquidate the capital again. As a result, VC firms are only interested in those ventures that promise a fast value growth and a definite road to exit. Today, VC investment activity ranges from early stage to very late stage startup funding, but scalability remains at the heart of the criteria to receive this kind of financing.

Other financing sources include family offices, corporate VC, and private equity firms. These are, however, irrelevant for most early stage and Berlin-based startups. Accelerator and incubator programs are very important for these startups and are discussed in Chap. 9.

PRACTICAL IMPLICATIONS FOR ENTREPRENEURS

So, what does all this mean for nascent entrepreneurs? How can they assess whether their business case is driven by scalability or by an SME mindset? And how do they get the investors to invest? The HIIG Startup Clinics provided various valuable insights into the challenges and opportunities that Berlin-based startups have. With a total of 81 sessions and 62 startups, the finance clinic was the second most frequented of the six clinic programs (see Table 6.1). I will discuss the key insights with regard to apparent prerequisites and supporting factors of raising capital from investors.

No Business Case? No Money!

A key lesson that many, especially first-time, entrepreneurs have to learn is that German investors exhibit little inclination to fund startups that have no business case. Several prominent US-based startups started out without any clear idea of how they would ever earn money with their product or service, and they received VC nonetheless. So-called "freemium" models (where a user gets a basic set of services for free but must pay in order to use extended "premium" functions) are a perfect example of how differently investors view startups. For some investors, a freemium approach represents a viable business model strategy; for others, it is merely a

Table 6.1   Source of information for finance clinic research stream

Number of startups	*Number of sessions*	*Startup phase*
62	81	35 × Early stage
		17 × Expansion stage
		10 × Steady stage

customer acquisition strategy that does not qualify as a business model, not to mention as a business case.

Many startups that participated in the Startup Clinics program faced a situation where they thought that they had a viable business model, but in fact lacked a comprehensive strategy of how to earn money. Unsurprisingly, these ventures struggled to convince investors to finance them. German investors in particular are conservative in respect of their investment strategy. For them, an essential prerequisites for considering investment is that the startup can present a thought-through and realistic business case that will—better sooner than later—yield a profit.

SME Mindsets Dominate

As discussed previously, scalability frequently qualifies as another prerequisite for financiers to invest. However, many founders who visited the Startup Clinics program exhibited an approach to company creation that can be best described as SME mindset driven. These entrepreneurs lack the experience or ambition necessary to build a scalable startup. Often business models are (too) conservative and traditional, focusing on national, or even local, niche markets, while disregarding existing international or blue ocean markets. Value propositions also tend to lack ambition and scalability—for example, owing to a focus on minor improvements to existing solutions instead of groundbreaking value creation in new services and products. This is very unappealing to investors who—owing to the high risk involved in startup funding—require potential high returns indicated by ambitious business plans. There is a fine line between an ambitious strategy to conquer (new) markets that appeals to investors and a business model that lacks a plausible road to profitability. The early stage funding gap described above is thus amplified by a missing fit between the young business's orientation and the investors' scope.

Liquidity Is Key

Over the course of 81 sessions with very young and young startups, it was observed that only a few had any notion of key performance indicators (KPIs) and some were not even aware of their fundamental importance and existence. This can be traced back to a lack of business know-how that in fact marked many Startup Clinic startups and their founders. Most importantly—and surprisingly—a good number of entrepreneurs came into a session to discuss their financial situation and did not know about their startup's liquidity.

The amount of money that the entrepreneurs have at their disposal—that is, money that is not tied up—is essential to react to foreseen and unforeseen events (and bills). It is also relevant for a startup's runway. Runway describes the time it has left until the venture runs out of money. A typical and frequent inquiry in the Finance Clinic was:

> We have only a few weeks left of EXIST—and we need venture capital funding—or something similar (Founders, early stage startup)

Such statements are of course naïve and demonstrate a neglect of financial common sense. Liquidity ought to be at the top of any entrepreneur's list of priorities, and it does not necessarily have to rely on new investments coming in. Various startups participating in the Startup Clinics took micro-loans from Berlin's state-owned investment bank IBB while others engaged in project-based partnerships that helped to pay the bills. While this is not ideal—it might distract the team from developing the core product—such a strategy allows for the extension of the available runway, and might thus help to secure the startup's survival.

Plan Ahead and Consider Lead Times

This is not to say that venture should not build on external capital. Raising BA or VC greatly leverages a startup's options in terms of expansion, product development, and market penetration. Entrepreneurs ought to schedule for lead times that range from a few weeks up to half a year until a deal is made. Startups that are in danger of running out of money during this time face two challenges. First, their bargaining power is substantially weakened as they desperately need money to survive. Second, investors—and professional ones in particular—require a set amount of time to check and verify the startup's situation. If this due diligence cannot be performed, financiers will opt against the investment.

Startups can prepare for many of the steps that a deal passes through, and thus reduce lead times. Usually, investors will base their decision on whether or not to engage with a venture on its pitches, its presentations about itself, and its plans. A pitch deck, for example, is a big part of a pitch and can be carefully prepared in advance. Ideally, this summarizes the business opportunity: it covers the business case as well as the way value is being created and how relevant customer needs are satisfied (the business model). A pitch deck should cater to the investor's existing knowledge about the startup and its market. In fact, several startups asked for help with just this:

> Can you help us with our pitch deck? We have several meetings with investors lined up. (Founders, expansion stage startup)

Social Capital Leads to Venture Capital

Most early stage investors are people of independent means who are embedded in and value private social networks. Startup founders often asked where they might find investors. Various BA associations exist—the Business Angel Club Berlin, for instance—but these tend to agglomerate inexperienced investors. Informal networks seem to be of greater importance. These are constituted by multiple joint investments by two angels and depend heavily on personal sympathy and appreciation. For startups, such networks are often obscure and difficult to identify. Entrepreneurs who lack relevant personal networks of their own must thus pitch at meetings that investors may or may not attend. Early stage startups in particular have a hard time because they have little to demonstrate and no relationships to mentors or investors:

> Where and how do I find investors? Our startup needs money to develop a beta version of our product. (Founders, early stage startup)

For more seasoned startups, social capital is also based in existing investors. Growth stage startups that seek VC would be well advised to motivate their current investors to participate in approaching financing rounds as well. This represents an endorsement of the startup by investors who have known the team and its performance for some time—thus increasing the chance that new investors provide VC to fund the startup's next development phase.

THE BERLIN CASE: HYPE VERSUS REALITY

How does the situation for Berlin-based startups look on a more abstract level—both at the moment and in future? According to startup news network TechCrunch, Berlin was "the fastest-growing startup ecosystem in the world and received the most venture capital investment of any city in Europe" in 2015 (TechCrunch, 2016). Bloomberg Businessweek described the Berlin hype process as: "First came the artists, then came the DJs, and then came the entrepreneurs" (Bloomberg Businessweek, 2016). In 2015, Berlin pooled close to 2 billion Euros of VC financing—an estimated 69 % of all such financing in Germany (Kahl & Scheuplein, 2016).

But what does that entail for Berlin based startups? Surprisingly, very little from a financial perspective. Most external and private funding is funneled into relatively few ventures. Those that receive substantial amounts are extremely professional, seasoned, and often not German. For example, take the VC superstars Rocket Internet (a startup factory that throws up new ventures on a weekly basis) or Soundcloud (a music streaming service that relocated to Berlin from Stockholm in 2007).

The Ecosystem Relies on Public Funding

From an ecosystem perspective, however, this financial influx likely attracts more entrepreneurs to found in and startups to relocate to Berlin. The reliance of these ventures on public subsidies remains high, though, because there are insufficient numbers of private early stage financiers. Though the German capital hosts 68 % of the nation's accelerator and incubator programs (Kahl & Scheuplein, 2016), Berlin lacks a vibrant BA and family office scene.

Public programs attempt to fill this funding gap with varying degrees of success. Public spending is usually not as efficient as private spending and research on the effect subsidies have on startups has not yet yielded any clear results. Indications vary, from suggesting a very positive effect of early stage subsidies on survival rates of startups to the possibly detrimental effects on startup development that Egger, Eggert, Keuschnigg, and Winner (2010) found. An over-reliance on subsidies hinders market-oriented behavior by the startup, reminiscent of life support rather than the jump starting of a highly scalable new venture.

The Road Ahead

As more nascent entrepreneurs found, fail, and try again, they probably become more experienced in what it takes to build a scalable and thus fundable startup. In the USA, serial entrepreneurs are more likely to receive external financing if they learned from past failures (see also Chap. 2). New investors appreciate that previous investors paid for past mistakes.

German investors seem to lack this insight, and failed serial entrepreneurs have to overcome this stigma.

With more exits on the way, two effects will come into play. First, returns on investment are generated for BA and VC investors, which increases the likelihood of follow-up investments and larger funds. Secondly, startup founders and vested employees with equity shares yield substantial capital gains in case of liquidity events. These entrepreneurs can then become experienced BAs who fund startups similar to their own.

CONCLUSION

In the case of Berlin, we can observe a steep but heavily skewed increase of external and private venture funding. We also need to differentiate between different kinds of new business creations, most notably future SMEs and scalable startups. This determines the sources of capital that are available to a nascent company. Only scalable startups are candidates for private financing from BA and VC investors.

Startups have a myriad of tools at their disposal to convince investors and increase their chance of receiving funding—but they also need to recognize established prerequisites that financiers expect from them. A compelling business case, well-managed KPIs, and social capital (see Chap. 2) are among the most important ones, and greatly support a startup's fundraising efforts. But we must also not forget that professional and deep pocket investors are thin on the Berlin ground owing to the local ecosystem's relative immaturity. Instead, public funding by government bodies dominates early stage startup support—both financially and non-financially. But this might only be so at the present time. With more exits and liquidity events, the financing scene will most likely mature in a way that existing investors continue to invest and new ones enter the game. With regard to the hype surrounding Berlin as a new European startup center, we face a situation in which more founders are indeed creating new businesses. But these businesses often do not qualify as scalable startups. It thus seems fair to say that founding a startup might be overhyped, but funding one is not.

REFERENCES

Blank, S. (2014). *Why companies are not startups*. Retrieved from https://steve-blank.com/2014/03/04/why-companies-are-not-startups/

Bloomberg Businessweek. (2016). *Berlin's startup hub wants to prove it's more than just a scene.* Retrieved from https://www.bloomberg.com/news/articles/2016-07-28/berlin-s-startup-hub-wants-to-prove-it-s-more-than-just-a-scene

Davila, A., Foster, G., & Gupta, M. (2003). Venture capital financing and the growth of startup firms. *Journal of Business Venturing, 18*(6), 689–708.

DSM. (2015). *Deutscher Startup Monitor 2016.* Berlin, Germany: BVDS & KPMG.

Duhautois, R., Redor, D., & Desiage, L. (2015). Long term effect of public subsidies on start-up survival and economic performance: An empirical study with French data. *Revue d'Économie Industrielle, 1,* 11–41.

Egger, P., Eggert, W., Keuschnigg, C., & Winner, H. (2010). Corporate taxation, debt financing and foreign-plant ownership. *European Economic Review, 54*(1), 96–107.

Fairchild, R. (2011). An entrepreneur's choice of venture capitalist or angel-financing: A behavioral game-theoretic approach. *Journal of Business Venturing, 26*(3), 359–374.

Kahl, J., & Scheuplein, C. (2016). *Berliner Venture-Capital Report 2016.* Berlin, Germany: Technologiestiftung Berlin.

Manolova, T. S., Manev, I. M., Carter, N. M., & Gyoshev, B. S. (2006). Breaking the family and friends' circle: Predictors of external financing usage among men and women entrepreneurs in a transitional economy. *Venture Capital, 8*(02), 109–132.

OECD. (2014). *OECD work on science, technology and industry.* Paris: OECD Publishing.

PWC. (2015). *Venture capital investing exceeds $17 billion for the first time since Q4 2000.* Retrieved from http://www.pwc.com/us/en/press-releases/2015/venture-capital-investing-exceeds.html 2016/01/23

PWC. (2016, January 16). *Historical trend data from the Money Tree Report.* Retrieved from http://www.p-wcmoneytree.com/HistoricTrends/Custom QueryHistoricTrend

Schramm, D. M., & Carstens, J. (2014). Eine kurze Geschichte der Unternehmensfinanzierung. In D. M. Schramm & J. Carstens (Eds.), *Startup-Crowdfunding und Crowdinvesting: Ein Guide für Gründer* (pp. 1–4). Wiesbaden, Germany: Springer.

TechCrunch. (2016). *How Berlin can become Europe's No. 1 tech hub.* Retrieved from https://techcrunch.com/2016/07/07/how-berlin-can-become-europes-no-1-tech-hub/

CHAPTER 7

Why Business Model Innovation Matters to Startups

Martina Dopfer

Abstract Business model innovation is a popular topic in academia and practice. This chapter examines why business model innovation should matter to Internet-enabled startups. The results stem from a qualitative research project, which was embedded in the Startup Clinics on Business Models run by the Alexander von Humboldt Institute for Internet and Society (see Chap. 3). The one-on-one sessions and workshops provided founders with a platform to address challenges around their business models. Based on the observation of three years of Startup Clinic sessions, the author derived three insights into the relationship of startups and the process of business model innovation. These insights show that startups struggle to align their business models coherently, particularly in the early phases. At the same time, their founders' backgrounds and experiences have a critical influence on the design of the business model. The author recommends that startups employ systematic approaches to business model innovation.

Keywords Business model innovation • Startups • Business model research • Core elements of a business model • Multiple case study

---

M. Dopfer (✉)
Alexander von Humboldt Institute for Internet and Society, Berlin, Germany

© The Author(s) 2018
N. Richter et al. (eds.), *Entrepreneurial Innovation and Leadership*,
https://doi.org/10.1007/978-3-319-71737-1_7

History and Background

The Internet has enabled the development of many new business models. Uber, for example, has become one of the biggest providers of shared car services globally. Similarly, Airbnb has grown into one of the biggest platforms offering holiday stays without owning a single apartment. In other words, the Internet offers startups a way to easily and rapidly test, prototype, and iterate new ways of offering and delivering value. It facilitates customer reach and feedback and helps to quickly adapt first product or service prototypes accordingly.

To understand how startups conceptualize and develop their business models, the Alexander von Humboldt Institute for Internet and Society conducted its own empirical research within Berlin's flourishing startup ecosystem. This was accompanied by extensive review of the existing literature on startup business models (Wirtz, Pistoia, Ullrich, & Göttel, 2016). In the course of supporting startups in the process of ideation, definition, or refinement of their business models, the researcher and author uncovered valuable findings regarding the development of startup business models:

- From the very beginning, startups struggle to establish a coherent business model.
- Founders' backgrounds and experiences are critical to a startup's initial business model design.
- Systematic approaches to business model innovation can be used to support startups in formulating, iterating, and enhancing their business models.

How Startups Find and Create Their Business Models: Theoretical Background

The management literature describes various streams of business model and business model innovation (Gassmann, Frankenberger, & Csik, 2014). However, scholars generally agree that business models are directly related to any startup's competitive advantage. Business models provide particular advantages to first movers and contribute positively to a company's overall performance (Chesbrough, 2010).

Scholars also agree that business models are shaped by both internal and external factors (Zott & Amit, 2015), which connect the company to their environment and help to establish clear boundaries. In addition, business models explain how companies interact with their stakeholders. The creation of a business model is a crucial step in starting up a business.

Put differently, startups need to identify how they will propose, create, and capture value through their business models. Therefore it is important to clearly identify and articulate its core elements or dimensions. While many scholars agree on this threefold structure, Gassmann et al. (2014) find that the business model is defined by the following dimensions:

WHO: Who are the central customers and what are their needs?

WHAT: What is the unique value proposition, that is, the core offering of the company?
        (Value proposition)

HOW: How will the company deliver value through its resources and capabilities?
        (Value capture)

VALUE: How does the company capture value through the revenue model? Which costs need to be covered?
        (Value creation)

The author applied these four dimensions of a business model to guide her research. According to Demil and Lecocq (2010) the business model construct can be perceived in two ways: as a *static* construct that relies on the inherent logic of its respective dimensions, or as a *dynamic* vehicle that supports companies in managing change through strategic innovation of its dimensions. Consequently, *business model innovation* refers either to the innovation of an established business model, or to the development of a completely new business model (Chesbrough, 2010; Zott & Amit, 2015). The static and dynamic viewpoints both apply to startups: Internet-enabled startups, in particular, need to develop and settle upon a business model that works for them. The Internet makes it possible for startups to quickly start their businesses. It is easy to design a first version of a website, offer a (beta-) product, and get feedback from first customers and users. The feedback and flexible technology, in turn, help startups to iteratively adapt their business models. While the Internet makes it comparatively affordable and easy to start a business, it also demands and enables alterations to the startup's original business model. An important question in this context, and the research question behind this chapter, is:

> Why do business models and business model innovation matter to (Internet) startups?

BUSINESS MODEL RESEARCH

To answer the stated research question, the author chose a qualitative research design and worked with a multiple case study method, which focused in depth on six startup cases. The goal was to gather insights supporting entrepreneurs facing the challenge of creating a functioning business model for their companies.

The startups were asked to complete a questionnaire concerning their business model, their current development stage, their founders, and the current challenges for their business models.

All except one of the startups in the study were in their early stages, having legally established their businesses in the previous three to twelve months. Five of the startups had initial ideas about their product and/or service, two of their revenue model, and around three of their target customer. Some had also asked friends or first customers to try out their product prototypes. Usually, the startups had received first financial funding through friends and family, and/or business angels. In addition, some of the startups had participated in an acceleration or incubation program through which they had received financial support, office space, and other services (e.g. mentoring). Most of the startups had one founder (two out of six) or a team of founders (four out of six) that shared tasks such as business development, information technology (IT), finance, and sales.

Based on the information provided, the author met with the startups either for one-on-one sessions or as part of a business model workshop. Almost all of the one-on-one sessions were dedicated to a business model-related challenge the startup currently faced. Workshops were offered to a maximum of ten startups. Sessions and workshops both followed the subsequent structure (Gassmann et al., 2014):

- *initiation*: establishing business model challenges,
- *ideation*: creating ideas for the business model,

- *integration*: bringing the ideas into a business model framework,
- *implementation*: developing a plan for implementing the new business model.

All conversations were recorded in writing, and photographs were used to ensure reliable documentation throughout. Startups were further asked for supplementary information such as pitch decks and business plans, and the author also queried databases such as online newspapers or "Angels List" for additional secondary data. The raw data was analyzed for emerging patterns, and themes and repeated keywords were identified for semantic coding. Subsequently, initial themes were identified and set in the context of the theoretical background informing the study. The initial startup business models are summarized in Table 7.1. Additional startup information and their most urgent questions around the business model are depicted in Table 7.2.

FINDINGS

Three main themes emerged from the data. First, many startups struggle to align their business model dimensions. In fact, they tend to focus primarily on one or two dimensions and forget about others. Founder 1 emphasizes: "The most important thing for me and my startup is to develop a well-working product." Similarly, Founder 2 explains: "I have been working in this industry for many years. So I know which revenue models work and I did not bother to look too much into other possible revenue models." Notably, founders tend to put a lot of energy and effort into one specific dimension of the business model, such as the "who" or the "what." The theory argues that entrepreneurs contemplate opportunities in relation to the perceived priority of their business model dimensions during the stages of venture creation or change. Yet a successful business model lives from the compelling logic contained in the integration of all business model dimensions (Zott & Amit, 2015). Hence, the evidence in this study suggests that startups often lack the knowledge and awareness to establish a comprehensive business model in their early stages.

Second, as founders are usually the ones who conceive the initial business idea, it is also they or their founder team who shape the first business model. The data shows that founders with more technical backgrounds

Table 7.1 Overview of cases

Startup	Who	What	Value	How
Startup 1	Reader of popular science books under time pressure	Short abstracts of books available via smartphone application and audio	Subscription model	Download through app stores; partner distribution; online marketing
Startup 2	E-commerce platforms	Platform for optimizing online advertising through a software-as-a-service product	Signup fee; license fee	Consulting to enable customers to use the software; setup; direct selling; strategic account management
Startup 3	Senior citizens with special traveling needs	Traveling for seniors; tailored offers	Share of traveling costs; broker fee	Website; personal counseling; collaboration with partners (hotels, bus companies, travel agencies)
Startup 4	Landlords, house owners, people renting their homes	Simple change of providers through an online platform (electricity, gas, etc.)	Share of changing provider's fee – affiliate model; working with preferred partners	Providers as partners; online marketing; after sales; yearly recommendations for customers
Startup 5	Sustainability oriented, environmentally conscious consumers	Platform for sale of sustainable products	Affiliate model	Website as matching platform of supply and demand worldwide
Startup 6	Students, professional beginners	Matching flatmates in selected cities worldwide	Affiliate model; partnering with landlords	Website as matching platform; partners for distribution of offer

put a lot of emphasis on enhancing their products and services as opposed to founders with industry-related backgrounds, who are more market- and customer-focused. For instance, Founder 1, a former IT developer, holds that "our main focus at the moment is programming our platform." Founder 4 explains: "I have been working with many big telecommunications customers for a long time. I just know that they don't know how to analyze their data systematically." This finding is supported by other research

Table 7.2   Questions around the business model

Startup	Stage	Team size	Business model question	Internet-enabled
Startup 1	Mid–later-stage	<20	Is the current business model scalable?	Yes
Startup 2	Early–mid-stage	<15	Should we go for a two-sided business model?	Yes
Startup 3	Early stage	<8	How do we reach our customer group?	Yes
Startup 4	Early stage	<20	How should we define our revenue model?	Yes
Startup 5	Early–mid-stage	<10	We are looking for Series A investors and would like you to challenge our business model before doing so.	Yes
Startup 6	Early stage	<5	What could be a working revenue model?	Yes

holding that business models originate in the founders' minds. The academic research confirms that startups adapt their business models according to the entrepreneur's background and environmental changes (Cavalcante, Kesting, & Ulhøi, 2011). Essentially, the findings demonstrate that founders, their backgrounds, and their perception of what is important are the core drivers to designing the startup's business model.

Third, during the Startup Clinics on Business Models, founders and/or founder teams displayed recurring behaviors: Founder 5 stated: "We don't usually sit down and brainstorm on the entire business model." Founder 3 added: "To me, the business model is the revenue model. I never considered the other dimensions and tried to bring it all together." Lastly, Founder 4 explained: "Ideating on business models really helped me see our customers and market from a different perspective." This demonstrates that startups and their founders act under a lot of pressure. Business model development, which requires systematic attention but does not have the urgency of other everyday demands, can be neglected or sacrificed. Pressure may stem from first investors, who demand high and quick customer growth and recurring revenues. Instead of articulating their carefully thought-through and explicitly designed business models, startups are forced to report to their investors on key performance indicators such as revenues and customers on a weekly or monthly basis. Yet it is vital to startups to pay consistent attention to systematic business model design (Zott & Amit, 2015). Only in this way might they be able to ensure the establishment of a functioning and scalable business model that aligns all the required dimensions. This business model would also serve as a boundary object, helping to facilitate both internal and external communication and supporting the development of common understandings, an effective value chain, and decisions and actions that are aligned.

IMPLICATIONS FOR STARTUPS

First, founders, employees, and stakeholders engaged in business model creation need to be aware of all four dimensions of "who," "what," "how," and "value," and how they interact within their business model. As the evidence has shown, startups should consciously and constantly iterate and innovate their business models. Often, however, they fail to do so owing to various reasons, such as a lack of time or competing, more pressing needs. Working with visual methods can be an easy way to meet those constraints. Visual methods can include the following boards:

- A *vision board* that includes the startup's vision, mission, biggest challenge, and next steps.
- A *timetable board* that depicts the five major milestones over the upcoming six months.
- A *value proposition canvas*, which addresses the main customer, and their pains and gains.
- A *business model canvas* that explains the main business model dimensions ("who," "what," "how," and "value") in full detail.
- A *key learnings* board with the biggest hindrances and failures the startup has experienced so far.

Those boards should decorate the office walls of every startup. In this way, the startup is constantly reminded of its vision, milestones, business model, and key learnings. In addition, boards are flexible tools that can be updated constantly, for example during weekly management meetings. Easy iterations become possible and accessible to all startup members. Meanwhile, the startup creates a shared internal understanding and an aligned external communication to stakeholders.

Second, founders should take time to reflect upon and assess their own backgrounds and experience, intentions, and objectives. This helps to identify how their personal priorities might impact the design of their business models, and may prevent this focus leading to a one-dimensional plan. Exchange with experts such as business coaches, angels, or co-founders could be helpful. In a best-case scenario, the founders find a way to engage one or two experts on a regular (weekly, monthly) basis for a longer period. To do so, they can negotiate a paid coaching plan for a certain time. Another option could be to offer discounted shares, thus making the experts business angels or investors with an early buy-in. Option two especially will increase the motivation of an expert to dedicate time and thought to the startup. Additionally, founders could consider hiring co-founders or employees who complement their own experiences.

Third, startups could adopt the approach used by the Startup Clinics on Business Models, which employ a systematic framework to develop, design, and innovate business models. Exchanges with startups from different industries have also proven to benefit cross-fertilization. It is recommended to organize such cross-industry exchanges along previously agreed on questions and challenges. This way, the exchange participants know what to expect and can prepare their input accordingly. In addition, a designated facilitator, who could be an expert on or coach to one of the attending startups, should ensure the exchange closes with precise key takeaways and next steps.

REFERENCES

Cavalcante, S., Kesting, P., & Ulhøi, J. (2011). Business model dynamics and innovation: (Re) establishing the missing linkages. *Management Decision, 49*(8), 1327–1342.

Chesbrough, H. (2010). Business model innovation: Opportunities and barriers. *Long Range Planning, 43*(2–3), 354–363.

Demil, B., & Lecocq, X. (2010). Business model evolution: In search of dynamic consistency. *Long Range Planning, 43*(2), 227–246.

Gassmann, O., Frankenberger, K., & Csik, M. (2014). *The business model navigator: 55 models that will revolutionise your business.* Harlow, UK: Pearson Education Ltd.

Wirtz, B. W., Pistoia, A., Ullrich, S., & Göttel, V. (2016). Business models: Origin, development and future research perspectives. *Long Range Planning, 49*(49), 36–54.

Zott, C., & Amit, R. (2015). Business model innovation: Toward a process perspective. In *The Oxford handbook of creativity, innovation and entrepreneurship: Multilevel linkages* (pp. 395–406). New York: Oxford University Press.

CHAPTER 8

How Established Firms Can Profit from Working with Startups

Paul Jackson, Nancy Richter, and Thomas Schildhauer

Abstract There are substantial differences in the objectives, working culture and work practices of established companies and startups, and these differences have, until now, been little researched. This chapter presents the most important differences in order to demonstrate how these may influence the ability of these firms to work together to produce successful innovations that benefit both parties. Such differences include attitudes to risk, change and the future. Interviews were conducted with representatives from 20 firms engaged in collaborative projects. The interviews were directed at understanding their objectives in the partnerships, the structural properties of the collaboration, working culture and processes, and the work environment. The results showed specific and common, though not universal, differences, which lead to divergent expectations and behaviour, and therefore provide a basis for improving the partnership.

Keywords Startups • Established firms • Successful collaboration • Belief systems

P. Jackson (✉)
Edith Cowan University, Joondalup, WA, Australia

N. Richter • T. Schildhauer
Alexander von Humboldt Institute for Internet and Society, Berlin, Germany

© The Author(s) 2018
N. Richter et al. (eds.), *Entrepreneurial Innovation and Leadership*,
https://doi.org/10.1007/978-3-319-71737-1_8

Background

Current rates of innovation, competition and economic change are higher than ever before, placing companies under significant pressure to develop new products, services, approaches to marketing and production methods (see also Chap. 1). In particular, disruptive innovations in the Internet are allowing powerful new entrants, such as Google and Amazon, to quickly establish a market presence and challenge incumbent market leaders and players. These companies introduce new concepts and models which disrupt entire industries, such as manufacturing or finance (Wirtz, Schilke, & Ullrich, 2010). The barriers to entry through the Internet are very low: cloud services, infrastructure as a service or e-commerce building blocks are cheap, fast and ubiquitous. Internet-based companies are introducing new products, services and ways of operating at an accelerating rate, with all the advantages of the broad reach of the Internet, the economies of scale, automation and low capital requirements. Contemporary examples for the entry of new firms such as these are Google's driverless car, a threat to the car industry, or Amazon Fresh, whose same-day fresh food delivery may turn the food industry on its head. Established firms are compelled to confront these radical incursions by new companies or industry outsiders and take the impact of the Internet, mobile computing, social media and other related technology platforms seriously.

Open innovation is one approach that allows established firms to use the creativity of external parties in their own interest (Chesbrough, 2004). It can introduce precisely the kind of 'out-of-the-box' thinking that is required to meet these new challenges. Universities, customers and start-ups can be integrated into an 'outside-in' innovation process, in which these groups bring new ideas into the firm, or into 'inside-out' processes, in which internal requirements and ideas are developed collaboratively with external partners (Gassmann & Enkel, 2006). Other means of generating and integrating new ideas include conventional methods such as mergers and acquisitions or internal research and development (R&D) departments. One study showed however that the most successful companies are 37 % more likely to use open innovation than less successful companies.

An increasing number of companies are seeking to work with startups, which are young or nascent growth-oriented companies which base their solutions on highly scalable business models and high rates of innovation and flexibility. They are creative, risk-oriented and highly motivated—precisely the characteristics which encourage radical innovation (Vahs & Brem, 2015). Radical innovation involves new-to-market elements in function and cost-saving. Such innovations are usually introduced by new entrants (such as startups) and are at the core of entrepreneurial activity (Schumpeter, 1975).

Differences Between Startups and Established Firms

Cooperation between established firms and startups has advantages for both sides. Because startups are less committed to existing paradigms and move in the 'new world' of technologies and behaviour, they develop surprising and original ideas and approaches to problems of production or distribution. They can help existing firms to recognize opportunities for and threats to the products they develop. Furthermore, they bring an entrepreneurial spirit and often have specialized technical knowledge and particular talents; and they are agile and react flexibly to change (Galvan et al., 2014). On the other side, established firms bring experience, finance and an established network which can include potential new customers (Song, Podoynitsyna, van der Bij, & Halman, 2008). With support like this, startups can focus on their core ideas and profit from sales and marketing channels and resources (see Chap. 2).

Apart from the direct contribution of radical innovations, existing firms also develop relationships to groups which become future partners and suppliers, they support entrepreneurial thinking within their firm, and bring new and stimulating ways of approaching problem situations (see Chap. 1).

Whether deliberately or not, startups use the lean startup method or variations of it (Richter, Schildhauer, & Schneider 2015; Ries, 2011). Where established firms usually aim for efficiency and reliability in their approaches to projects and product delivery, startups work with higher uncertainty and low product maturity—so changes in direction are more likely, indeed sought after (Furr & Dyer, 2014). Eric Ries's lean startup consists of the three elements: build, measure, learn. A first version of a product is built called the 'minimum viable product', after which customers test and use the product. They give feedback, which is collected, measured and analysed, and from what is learned a new cycle of improvement is initiated, using the same steps. This results in the rapid, iterative development with tight feedback which result in high customer and market fit. Lean startup processes are fast and light, and involve few costs. Rather than use extensive market surveys, customers are consulted directly. Rather than a long-winded, linear development process which is broken down into specific phases with certain deliverables and features, teams can change direction and 'pivot' quickly as they repeat the same cycle until the right fit is found. This development process suits startups, acting as they do in an environment of high uncertainty—uncertainty of needs and outcomes, both in product features and business model operations.

At the beginning of a startup product lifecycle, there is often little history or knowledge of customer needs. Hypotheses must be made which guide startups in anticipating how customers might respond to the product or service functionality. The lean startup cycle serves to test these hypotheses and does it quickly. Hypotheses are not ideas that are held dear (in contrast to much traditional product design): the underlying principle is usually 'fail fast, fail early'. The first product versions from startups often resemble unfinished and unpolished prototypes—the customer is the focus and is integrated in the development cycle as quickly as possible. On the basis of their feedback, the product assumptions are constantly questioned and the product improved. In particular with Internet services, updates are very simple; and pivots are encouraged when the product is not meeting market needs. Therefore, in the most fundamental processes of product development there are substantial differences between established companies and startups; and behind these processes in large firms there are roles, responsibilities, careers and deeply held beliefs about what constitutes a rational approach to new product development.

Such development processes are not the only areas where there are differences between startups and established firms, but it is clear that such differences involve differences in beliefs and ways of thinking that could hinder cooperation. Our analysis of the data we collected in many interviews with startups and established firms engaged in such 'partnerships' show significant differences which can lead to misunderstanding, inappropriate mutual assessments and ultimately decisions and behaviour which damage the collaboration. Some of these are listed in Table 8.1.

Table 8.1   The different belief systems of startups and firms

Concept	Attitude of startups	Attitude of established firms
The future	The future is totally different to the past	The future is pretty much like the past
Risk	Risks must be taken	Risks are to be avoided
Time	Available time is short	Available time is whatever the plan says
Personal goals	I want to build a company	I want to be in a company
Self-efficacy	I am in control	I have some control
Identification with the product	This is my product	This is the company's product
Success	I am responsible for success	I play a role in success

Examples adapted from Jackson and Richter (2017)

PATHWAYS TO SUCCESSFUL COLLABORATION

In spite of these differences, there are ways to facilitate successful collaboration. From the side of the established firms these are clear goals, careful planning, clear selection criteria and a well-organized search for the right startup partners, well-defined collaboration and management processes, an understanding in the firm of the required structures and attitudes (openness, flexibility, tolerance of difference) and management processes and governance which are directed towards delivering benefits to the firm, rather than a particular group. This overall process is shown in Fig. 8.1 and discussed in the following sections.

So what are the most important steps for established firms to take in developing a successful set of partnerships with startups?

Step 1: Develop Your Innovation Strategy

Some companies have an explicit innovation strategy, but few have a clear, enterprise-wide, long-term strategy on working with startups. Such cases often depend on an individual staff member and things are decided on a case-by-case basis. This makes them vulnerable to staff changes, reduces their chances of success and restricts the full organisational benefit. Because startups are usually even less clear on how to work with larger firms, there is great scope for confusion, misunderstanding and escalation of frustration. A clear strategy with budget allocations, measurable goals and governance processes will greatly increase the chances of success as well as encourage goal setting on the part of the startup.

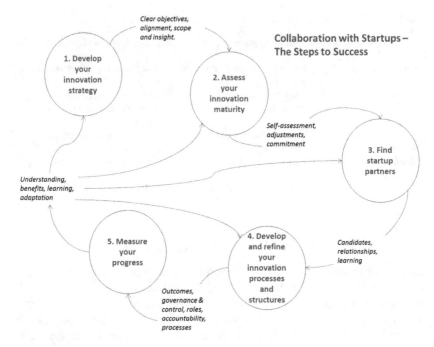

Clear objectives, alignment, scope and insight.

Collaboration with Startups – The Steps to Success

1. Develop your innovation strategy

2. Assess your innovation maturity

Self-assessment, adjustments, commitment

3. Find startup partners

Understanding, benefits, learning, adaptation

5. Measure your progress

4. Develop and refine your innovation processes and structures

Candidates, relationships, learning

Outcomes, governance & control, roles, accountability, processes

Fig. 8.1   Five steps to successful working with startups (From Jackson, Richter, & Morle, 2016)

Some of the questions that a company should typically ask itself include:

- What important and strategic problems do we need to solve?
- What do we expect from a collaboration with startups (culture change, long term suppliers, company image, employer branding, radical product ideas?)
- How urgent is this; how much pressure are we under?
- Do we have the cultural and managerial will and capability to make this work?
- How much do we want to invest?

Once these questions have been answered, a strategy for open innovation with startups can be developed. This strategy needs to become accepted, legitimated and articulated throughout the organisation to establish a standard mode of operation.

Step 2: Assess Your Innovation Maturity

Organisations need to prepare their organisations well to maximise the chances of success. A self-evaluation of its own internal capabilities will help organisations make decisions about their readiness to participate in such partnerships. Some of the following attributes, for example, will facilitate collaboration with startups:

- A strategic repositioning of the firm—new markets, business growth, new brand or new business models. As an example, BMW aims to be a leader in 'individual premium mobility' – not just making luxury cars. For this it seeks to use digital technologies to connect people, vehicles and services. Such a strategic repositioning opens up BMW for cooperation with partners who are in a position to think outside the box and allows them to combine incremental and radical innovation.
- Clear executive management support and involvement—without the support of top management, cooperation with startups will bring no sustainable advantages to an organisation. At least one senior manager must be directly responsible for this strategy.
- A focus on shared value and not just a need for a supplier to provide defined services—cooperating with startups should not be used as a method to utilise creative subcontractors. It is much more about the creation of a win–win partnership that requires a common understanding of the shared value, without which results are usually less than promising.
- Line management capability and motivation to make it work—without basic operational management competence and a motivation to use ideas from the outside, such collaborations do not work. The 'not invented here syndrome' can sabotage the best of externally sourced innovations and ideas. Managers and staff involved in these relationships must be educated in the formal and motivational aspects of these partnerships and held to account according to clear performance criteria.
- An organisational ability to absorb new knowledge and make the most of it—organisations must recognise that particular competencies and processes are required to absorb ideas from the outside and take them through to be ready for market.
- Organisational awareness and mindfulness of what is going on in the firm—this is needed to identify problems (and opportunities) early and pass them on to who should know or can do something about

them: good internal maps of who knows what, who needs to know what, what processes need to be initiated at what time, respect for competency irrespective of hierarchical position; in other words, a well-functioning, competent organisation in which staff are motivated to work towards organisational rather than individual goals.

- An ability to cope with ambiguity and uncertainty—this reflects capabilities to work with 'unknown unknowns', things not previously encountered, not just Knightian uncertainty, which is the absence of knowledge of probabilities. Such uncertainties encompass 'black swans' for example, concepts that simply in the past have never been combined. Managers need to be able to deal with, and consider the potential of, such recombination of knowledge that startups might introduce.

Organisational culture is a key capability for any open innovation undertaking. An organisational culture in which norms of openness, tolerance, risk-taking and creativity are present will have more chance of successfully executing and integrating the outcomes of open innovation projects than conservative, risk-avoiding, inward-looking companies. Overall, it is a good idea to take an honest look at oneself and conduct an objective assessment of your organisation's innovation maturity. Depending upon the outcomes of such a review, a change management process may be required to introduce behaviours and norms conducive to innovation and collaboration.

Step 3: Find Startup Partners

Startups often have no public profile and may be difficult to locate. Firms have several options in this search: they can utilise a seed or startup accelerator, which organises cohorts of startups with a focus on a particular industry or technology sectors (see Chap. 9); advertising or word of mouth in the appropriate media is a possibility; or they can employ a scout or venture capital form to find startups on their behalf.

Some examples of criteria for selecting and investing in a startup include:

- the startup is active in a new market area, with no existing competition or addresses the needs of a new class of consumers,
- the startup consists of an entrepreneurial, creative, well-balanced team,
- the startup possesses advanced technological knowledge.

Companies should be aware that there will be fundamental differences in the conventional assessment of a subcontractor or supplier and the typical situation of a startup: where a company normally expects its suppliers to have a track record, customer recommendations and be financially stable, the reality is that many startups have no finished product details, little experience with large companies and live from hand to mouth. And of course, unlike many conventional suppliers, a startup has an independent vision of where it wants its products to go.

Step 4: Develop and Refine Your Innovation Processes and Structures

Management policies, processes, roles and responsibilities will be needed to guide innovation with startups. A company needs to establish transparent structures, roles and management processes and provide clear interfaces and contact points to the startup. Therefore a company may even wish to set up separate independent management systems and organisational structures to support open innovation and provide an interface between innovation activities and the mother organisation.

- set up a governance structure, such as a steering committee, consisting of influential and authoritative managers who can guide open innovation projects in an appropriate way and provide organisational backing,
- formalise responsibilities such as contact persons, budgets, reporting and so on—perhaps even a special team or organisational grouping,
- define procedures for communication and work, project management and communications, including how the entrepreneurs will be selected,
- formulate clear contracts and agreements and establish a framework describing the duration, content and scope of the partnership,
- have a clear framework to manage the phases of discovery, incubation and acceleration and the transition between them.
- as necessary, try and change norms, attitudes and behaviour towards open innovation to be positive and embracing.

Step 5: Measure Your Progress

It is important to put in place measurement programmes that monitor the success of working with startups. You can measure input and output conditions for collaboration with startups and get an idea of the efficiency of your innovation efforts. Input capabilities and resources include:

- the level of support in the organisational culture, allowing time for innovation, nurturing the motivation to do so, rewarding success and allowing failure,
- the maturity of the processes and structures to support innovation,
- the management effort to work with startups and the number of people engaged,
- the time taken to move from idea to implementation,
- the cost and resources allocated to the startup projects.

It is crucial to measure and quantify the benefits to the firm in terms of innovation outputs. Measurable outputs might include:

- innovations created or the increase in internal entrepreneurial activities,
- the tangible payoff the organisation is getting in terms of savings, revenue, decrease in cycle times and so on,
- non-tangible benefits such as organisational learning, changes to organisational attitudes to innovation and culture arising from working with startups, or the attractiveness of the firm to new talent,
- the innovation maturity of your organisation using standard scales, for example from 'Basic' to 'Optimising'.

Combining input and output metrics will also give an idea of the efficiency of the process in generating the desired outcomes.

CONCLUSION

An increasing number of organisations are seeking to collaborate with startups. The reasons range from a desire to boost product innovation to the desire to make themselves more attractive to well-educated, talented young employees or to improve their image. These efforts often end in failure because established firms do not take a strategic and focused approach which articulates what they want to achieve. Wrong perceptions about startups are also a common cause for failure. The divergent cultures of startups and firms also influence the outcomes of such undertakings. For this reason it is important for any company to understand the differences between its own processes and behaviour and those of a startup, and have a clear idea of the success factors for collaboration. We hope that this chapter has provided an introduction to these differences and offers concrete recommendations on planning, implementing and overseeing such partnerships.

REFERENCES

Chesbrough, H. (2004). Managing open innovation. *Research-Technology Management, 47*(1), 23–26.

Furr, N., & Dyer, J. (2014). *The innovator's method*. Boston: Harvard Business Review Press.

Galvan, C., Gratzke, P., Jelinek, T., Kiessler, A., Nurluel, M., Quigley, J., et al. (2014). *Enhancing Europe's competitiveness – Fostering innovation-driven entrepreneurship in Europe*. Geneva, Switzerland: World Economic Forum.

Gassmann, O., & Enkel, E. (2006). Open innovation. *zfo Wissen, 3*(75), 132–138.

Jackson, P., & Richter, N. (2017). Situational logic: An analysis of open innovation using corporate accelerators. *International Journal of Innovation Management, 21*(7), 1–21.

Jackson, P., Richter, N., & Morle, P. (2016). Whitepaper: Working with startups. *Pollenizer*, 1–12. Available at http://www.pollenizer.com/working-with-startups/

Richter, N., Schneider, T., & Schildhauer, T. (2015). Projektgovernance in etablierten Unternehmen & digitalen start-ups. *Zeitschrift für Projektmanagement, PMaktuell, 2015*(2).

Ries, E. (2011). *The lean startup*. New York: Crown Publishing Group.

Schumpeter, J. A. (1975). *Capitalism, socialism and democracy*. New York: Harper and Row.

Song, M., Podoynitsyna, K., Van Der Bij, H., & Halman, J. I. (2008). Success factors in new ventures: A meta-analysis. *Journal of Product Innovation Management, 25*(1), 7–27.

Vahs, D., & Brem, A. (2015). *Innovationsmanagement: von der Idee zur erfolgreichen Vermarktung*. Stuttgart, Germany: Schäffer-Poeschel.

Wirtz, B. W., Schilke, O., & Ullrich, S. (2010). Strategic development of business models: Implications of the web 2.0 for creating value on the internet. *Long Range Planning, 43*(2), 272–290.

CHAPTER 9

Radical Innovation Using Corporate Accelerators: A Program Approach

Nancy Richter, Paul Jackson, and Thomas Schildhauer

Abstract Collaboration between startups and established firms often fail, not only because of the motivation or capability of the participants, but also because of a poor understanding of the required management processes. This chapter examines corporate accelerators from the perspective of program management process and provides a checklist for the construction of a suitable framework.

Keywords Radical innovation • Corporate accelerators • Program theory • Innovation strategy

Background

Research shows that radical innovations are often introduced into the market by entrepreneurs via newly created firms (Ahuja & Lampert, 2001). Established firms are generally superior in delivering incremental innovation, improving existing technologies and business models bit by

N. Richter (✉) • T. Schildhauer
Alexander von Humboldt Institute for Internet and Society, Berlin, Germany

P. Jackson
Edith Cowan University, Joondalup, WA, Australia

© The Author(s) 2018   99
N. Richter et al. (eds.), *Entrepreneurial Innovation and Leadership*,
https://doi.org/10.1007/978-3-319-71737-1_9

bit (see Chap. 1). Therefore a key to facilitating the introduction of radical innovation by established firms is to merge elements of the old and new economies by working with startups (see Chap. 8). Examples of firms that execute this strategy include Disney Accelerator (Techstars), Microsoft Ventures Accelerator Tel Aviv, Axel Springer Plug & Play, Barclays Accelerator (Techstars), Nike+ Accelerator (Techstars) and ProSiebenSat1 Accelerator.

But what is an accelerator program exactly? They are programs that begin with a competition in which anyone with a clever business idea can participate. Usually the competitors are startup teams, nascent firms that think their original idea is realistic and can grow quickly. These ideas are innovative, new to the market, and may have the potential to increase profits and market presence substantially (Blank & Dorf, 2012). If the young firm shows promise, usually during the founding or pre-founding phase, an established firm might take a share of equity by providing funding and resources for further development. However, an increasing number of organizations are choosing not to take this approach, as the acceptance rate by startups is too low.

The accelerator program invites groups of entrepreneurs to participate in a "boot camp" in which they are supported by mentors, workshops, education, and a network of experienced company founders and experts in finance, law, methods, or technology (Jackson, Richter, & Schildhauer, 2015). Within a highly structured framework and a tight schedule with fixed delivery and demonstration dates, the startups present provisional versions of their product. The whole process has a specific rhythm and milestones are not moved, allowing a rapid selection of the best ideas that can be conceptualized, prototyped, and presented in a specific timebox. Perhaps more importantly, ideas that are considered to be less promising are discarded early and with low sunk cost.

Corporate accelerators are a specific type of accelerator, which a company might run internally or using an external service provider.

> The emergence of the corporate accelerator appears to have arisen from a desire by many companies to bring themselves closer to innovation and gain access to windows on emerging technology, thus staving off the gale of creative destruction. (Hochberg, 2015, p. 24)

The objectives of companies in doing this may vary from serious new product development to public relations and image management. Consequently, the advantages vary widely as well, but generally companies hope to gain fresh ideas and raise the motivation of their own teams. Startups profit by very quickly gaining access to financial support or other resources such as expert networks, marketing channels, or other partners (Jackson & Richter, 2017). At first glance, this seems like an obvious win–win situation and, if standardized and proven, it could form part of a national approach to innovation. However, these programs are relatively new and unproven, and the partnerships are not without problems. Many such programs fail because the processes are unclear, because it doesn't work the way the established firms expect or demand, because startups have no interest in responding to wordy or restrictive tenders, or because the two parties differ so substantially in their work practices and culture that if even great ideas are developed the two are incapable of working together to co-develop anything.

It has already been noted in Chap. 8, that deep-seated attitudinal, structural, and cultural differences collide in these partnerships. Good processes can help to identify these differences, set up preventive measures, and respond quickly when things start to go wrong. Often the partnerships fail not because of a lack of good will or capability, but because of a lack of clear, well-thought-through program practices.

In the following sections accelerators are analyzed using the lens of program management. We discuss how to make them work using a formal taxonomy of program management derived from Gomm (2000). We fill this taxonomic framework with the experiences and lessons expressed by managers of accelerators, startups, and company innovation managers.

How Can Managers Implement Corporate Accelerator Programs within Their Own Organization?

The successful use of startups by other organizations, and the necessity to keep abreast of new developments in technology, challenges managers to consider how they might apply this approach themselves. But duplicating the success of others is not easy; one cannot simply imitate a set of processes and expect the same results. A standard checklist for program designers should help such managers consider where the accelerator approach might be adapted to fit the needs of their own firm. We use a program framework which has been used particularly successfully in health and social welfare programs. Before we do this, we briefly discuss program theory, in particular using a realist approach as described by Pawson and Tilley (2004). We do this because programs need to be implemented with a clear idea of what makes the program work, and whether the conditions to trigger successful outcomes are present. Understanding why something might or might not work helps managers to evaluate, improve, and successfully implement programs that are initiated to achieve specific goals.

PROGRAM THEORY AS AN AID TO IMPROVING DESIGN AND IMPLEMENTATION OF INNOVATION STRATEGY

Programs are social undertakings aimed at improving outcomes and thereby resolving a certain set of problems. They emerge from the mental models people have of those problematic, or conversely desirable, situations and their understanding of what causes them to occur. Poverty should be reduced, injustice rectified, infrastructure improved, and innovations produced. The programs that are developed to address these issues should be based upon an understanding of causes. In our case, a corporate accelerator is intended to boost the probably inadequate levels of radical innovation in established firms in order to protect the firm from external disruption by competitors and new entrants. Programs are directed towards a vision or objective and are a practical conceptualization of how this vision can be achieved. They are context specific and are introduced into existing social systems to achieve change. Any program intervention should, to a degree, throw an existing system off balance, enabling causal change that leads to desired results. The central question becomes what works for whom and in what circumstances. Introducing the same formal accelerator program into two different organizations may lead to very different results—a single feature of the context may lead to quite divergent outcomes. In the case of corporate accelerator programs these could be factors such as:

- capabilities and charisma of trainers and trainees (i.e. startups, firm managers, and accelerator managers),
- personal relations between participants,
- value that the organization really attaches to innovation,
- quality and type of inputs into the accelerator from the wider context, such as infrastructure, facilities, government support programs, and so on.

If an accelerator program is successful, or generates a positive vibe in an organization, the motivation and capabilities of the participants create a virtuous circle, which ultimately becomes self-sustaining: a new type of creative, can-do culture emerges. But for this, contextual factors such as management support, tolerance of failure, and risk-taking are important. Even beyond this, such programs take place within open systems and are connected to a wider environment: unexpected events, new political drivers, technical developments, or a change in personnel can all influence the trajectory of an accelerator program—the outcomes are not deterministic, although in retrospect they might seem to be. In particular, a program architect should always be aware that it is not the program features that directly cause changes to happen. Human agents participating in the processes are influenced by those features to change their behavior or make certain decisions: it is "the process of how subjects interpret and act upon the intervention stratagem" (Pawson & Tilley, 2004).

Programs can have intended and unintended consequences. A program architect should monitor outcomes as they occur in a program: in the case of accelerators, it is not about numbers and measures (although these are important); it is also about changes effected by the program on the environment and actors themselves. Changes might be observable in the behavior of staff, readiness of managers to pursue risk or give their staff space to experiment, different kinds of conversations and language: these changes to the underlying substance of the firm may have a significant and sustainable influence on a firm's competitiveness and innovation readiness. Whatever the outcomes are, they may differ from firm to firm, depending upon the starting position and contextual factors which influence the trajectory. Program architects need to observe and identify the conditions which cause good or bad outcomes, and manage these factors accordingly to avoid failure: there is no silver bullet.

> Programme building is [...] a matter of getting the right ingredients in place in the right setting to suit the needs of particular sets of consumers. (Pawson & Tilley, 2004, p. 10)

Corporate Accelerator Programs

In our interviews with experienced practitioners (12 interviews with established firms, 12 with startups, and three with accelerator managers) and analysis of the existing accelerator literature, we have identified many of the essential features of corporate accelerator programs. These features can be used by a program architect during the definition and planning of a corporates accelerator program.

The first question for a program manager or architect to ask of each program feature is whether it will work in that particular context. Simply implementing standard features is not an option. Any accelerator program should be adapted to local conditions, so that features such as a pitch night, the lean startup method (Ries, 2011), or the limited time frame will trigger mechanisms that inspire participants in the firm and the startup to commit to and deliver innovative ideas that support company strategy. Table 9.1 takes the key general components of programs and makes suggestions as to how a program architect might consider the specific organizational context when the corporate accelerator is established and run.

Table 9.1 Success factors of accelerator programs

Program component	Contextual aspects that will help the feature to work
Strategy	There must be a clearly defined objective for the corporate accelerator. All participants must be helped to understand and commit to this objective. This needs to be propagated across the organization. The organization can choose from a number of outcomes that an accelerator with startups can provide, but it must explicitly manage towards these. An overarching innovation strategy is necessary to legitimate and provide resources, but a specific strategy for the corporate accelerators and working with startups is also required.
Resources	Established firms should create clear organizational signposts and pathways for the startups to the relevant sources of knowledge, information, and data, and to the right customer and internal networks. Senior management commitment is a *sine qua non*: lip service and clichés will only service to increase cynicism. Senior leaders must provide resources, support the projects, and be seen to be involved.
Processes	The established firm should have the ability to determine the duration, content, and form of the accelerator program. A competition to select the best participants, a fixed program duration, the use of lean startup methodologies and rapid interactions, and feedback keep the pulse of development rapid and even, preventing energy-sapping pauses, minimizing wait time, and maintaining momentum—all embedded within a disciplined framework.
Structures	In setting up the project groupings, roles and responsibilities, it is better to separate the accelerator from the routines of the established firm. This is also important for internal corporate accelerators. Freed from internal procedures and a culture that might say "slow down, we can't do that here," participants in corporates accelerators will be more likely to apply themselves in unconventional ways and come up with the most interesting and radical contributions to the firm.

(*continued*)

Table 9.1 (continued)

Program component	Contextual aspects that will help the feature to work
Roles and responsibilities	There should be a project manager, who is responsible for controlling the entire accelerator process. This project manager should either be, or report directly to, a senior manager. The accelerator itself should be run by an experienced accelerator manager, with startup and corporate experience, who creates the necessary bridges between the company and startups. It is important not to perceive startups as sub-contractors, but as equal partners, with their own needs and legitimate objectives: a basic principle of interaction should be to seek win–win outcomes and shared goals, which should be revisited and adapted in a continuous, flexible process.
Environment	The attitudes, culture, and existing work practices of the established firm are decisive. A positive and supportive enterprise culture will simplify the interaction with the new partners and assist the acceptance of new products by management and staff. To develop a radically innovative product or service with startups is one thing; to integrate this into an existing product suite (which it might threaten), or marketing processes, or brand is quite another story.
Results	For startups, a total focus on the customer and the permanent, relentless pursuit of customer and market fit is crucial: this attitude needs to be adopted by the established firm. Companies should only further refine and develop ideas which are attractive to key stakeholders, such as customers or investors. Metrics which measure success and progress should be developed and refined as the firm gains more experience in the workings of radical innovation.

The following table presents questions which established firms should ask themselves prior to commencing a corporate accelerator. They are the result of several years of international research, participant observation of, and conversations with those involved in accelerator programs. They may provide useful food for thought for program architects seeking to successfully engage the creative energies of startups and provide useful outcomes for established firms (Table 9.2).

An accelerator program functions as a high-performance filter, through which ideas, teams, and skills are passed and which weeds out lackluster innovations, poorly functioning teams, and those without the capabilities to make things work. This minimizes sunk costs and uncer-

Table 9.2   A checklist for corporate accelerators

Program component	Questions when planning a corporate accelerator program
Strategy	What are the goals of the program?
	Do we have a corporate strategy for open innovation processes with startups?
Resources	What resources are available?
	Do we have the resources necessary to run a corporate accelerator?
	What additional resources will we need?
Processes	What processes have we planned?
	Will the process be similar to existing accelerator programs?
	Are the objectives consistent with the overall goals?
	What must we adapt?
Structures	How should we organize our program?
	Is our program spatially and organizationally separated from the existing routines of our company?
	Do we need to change anything in our internal reporting or management?
	How do we optimize the exchange of ideas between core business and the accelerator program?
Roles	What roles should we define for the program?
	Who has overall responsibility?
	Do we have senior management support?
	Do we have an experienced and independent accelerator manager?
	What exactly is the role of the targeted startups?
Environment	What is the environment provided by the firm and the environment within which the firm operates?
	Are we open to new ideas?
	Where do we generally get new ideas?
	Are we in a position to integrate externally sourced, radically new ideas?
Results	How do we know that we have achieved our goals?
	Who are the most important stakeholders, who can independently assess success?
	Are we considering our most important customers?
	Do we have hard data and measures for customer satisfaction with new products or accelerator program efficiency and effectiveness?

tainty. Strict processes, selection criteria, and fixed decision points and deadlines keep creativity "under control" and maximize relevance and potential. Whilst it sounds brutal, startups are often grateful for the imposed discipline and structure. Established companies find it easier to steer the processes and idea development in a direction which suits them and to minimize the time spent on unsuitable proposals. Motivated, talented people from different backgrounds working together under these conditions have the potential to develop radical innovations with applications for established firms.

Companies generally become more involved in the innovation process after proposals begin to take shape. In due course, the number of ideas is reduced—at the beginning of the program generally a large number of possible ideas are floated, and these are reduced bit by bit. Objective criteria should be developed in advance and applied to help select the best ideas. An accelerator program thereby becomes more than a filter: it is a communications interface between the established firms and the startups. The accelerator creates a highly competitive and controlled environment which facilitates refinement of ideas and selection for further collaboration with startups.

CONCLUSION

A lot has happened in innovation theory and processes. Corporate accelerators are a relatively new and a little researched innovation program, whose most important function is to help companies to recognize and adopt new approaches, ideas, and technologies in the face of competition from traditional sources as well as new market entrants. But there are other significant benefits—reputation and brand enhancement, building relationships with talented future suppliers, or even the creation of new markets. Most companies who co-operate with startups are particularly interested in radical innovation, usually because they are operating in markets that are particularly threatened by new Internet entrants: incremental innovation is not enough in their industry.

In this chapter we have presented the key aspects of corporate accelerators within a program management framework in order to help those companies wishing to establish such an approach. But implementation is always bound into an existing context and the same formal program features, introduced into two different firms, may have completely different outcomes. Therefore the key question in program design and implementation should be how we can make this work for us, given our people, processes and culture. This reflective and considered approach is quite different, more nuanced, and more likely to succeed than approaches that simply tick off "critical success factors."

REFERENCES

Ahuja, G., & Lampert, C. M. (2001). Entrepreneurship in the large corporation: A longitudinal study of how established firms create breakthrough inventions. *Strategic Management Journal, 22*(6–7), 521–543.

Blank, S., & Dorf, B. (2012). *The startup owner's manual.* Pescadero, CA: K&S; RanchInc.

Gomm, R. (2000). Would it work here? In R. Gomm (Ed.), *Using evidence in health and social care* (pp. 171–191). London: Sage.

Hochberg, Y. (2015). *Accelerating entrepreneurs and ecosystems: The seed accelerator model innovation policy and the economy* (Vol. 16). Chicago: University of Chicago Press.

Jackson, P., & Richter, N. (2017). Situational logic – An analysis of open innovation using corporate accelerators. *International Journal of Innovation Management,* 1750062.

Jackson, P., Richter, N., & Schildhauer, T. (2015). Open innovation with digital startups using corporate accelerators – A review of the current state of research. *ZPB Zeitschrift für Politikberatung, 7*(4), 152–159.

Pawson, R., & Tilley, N. (2004). *Realist evaluation.* London: Sage.

Ries, E. (2011). *The lean startup.* New York: Crown Publishing Group.

CHAPTER 10

Meeting the Innovation Challenge: Agile Processes for Established Organisations

Nancy Richter, Thomas Schildhauer, and Paul Jackson

Abstract Traditional methods of innovation and market research have failed to keep pace with growing global competition and rates of change. Organisations are seeking new ways of accelerating innovation, in effect becoming more like startups. In this final chapter we present some of these new approaches, focusing on the managerial aspects of four particular methods for generating innovation, including case studies, and the advantages and challenges of each method. We examine the lean startup method, Google's Design Sprint, hackathons and scrum.

Keywords Agile processes • Innovation • Lean Startup • Design Sprint • Scrum • Hackathon • Dropbox • Google • Scout24 • Deutsche Bahn

N. Richter (✉) • T. Schildhauer
Alexander von Humboldt Institute for Internet and Society, Berlin, Germany

P. Jackson
Edith Cowan University, Joondalup, WA, Australia

© The Author(s) 2018   109
N. Richter et al. (eds.), *Entrepreneurial Innovation and Leadership*,
https://doi.org/10.1007/978-3-319-71737-1_10

Introduction: Agile Processes and Innovation

The location and external networks of organisations are becoming increasingly important. The ability to form and manage relationships with educational, research and creative institutions is a core competency, and within these networks of relationships to scientists, startups or creatives, organisations encounter different approaches to innovation such as design sprints, scrum, agile project management and the lean startup. These approaches are of interest to established firms, because they are used in contexts in which creative and agile thinking is dominant. In other parts of this book (see Chaps. 1 and 8) we have emphasised that firms must find new methods and processes in product and service development. In this chapter, we give some examples of how firms have applied agile processes to support development in environments of uncertainty. These processes are often foreign to corporate approaches to research, development and innovation. A particular focus and managerial attention is required to integrate these approaches, such that they are effective and sustainable. So what are some of these methods? How should they be organised, what are the key features and how does one take the outcomes and transfer them into concrete projects?

Innovation Process: Lean Startup

In Chap. 8 we presented the lean startup approach of Eric Ries (2014). This approach is the most common development method employed by startups. After arriving at a clear business vision, the process involves idea generation, implementation (i.e. generally coding) and then immediate testing by customers, from whom data is gathered to learn and improve. These form the basis of a highly iterative trio of processes of build—measure—learn, which is performed until a product or service is achieved that finds customer acceptance. In the first phase of Lean Startup, an organisation develops a prototype, also known as a minimum viable product (MVP). The organisation then tests this prototype to establish whether the product is of sufficient interest to be worth developing further. Not only startups use this approach: Dropbox, a former startup in the area of cloud storage, uses the lean startup approach to include customers in its innovation processes (Business.com, n. d.) (Fig. 10.1).

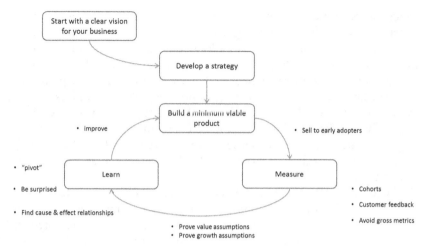

Fig. 10.1 The lean startup process

Case Study: Dropbox and Lean Startup

Dropbox was founded in 2007 by two Californian students with the objective of simplifying data transfer. In that year it was supported by the famous accelerator YCombinator. The beta phase of version 1.0 was introduced for private clients in 2010, and in 2011 Dropbox Business made storage capacity available to be purchased for teams. After a further test phase, Dropbox introduced a collaboration tool with which users could collaboratively develop and process text. In all its innovations, Dropbox followed the lean startup methodology.

In the early stages of founding, before it brought the official product onto the market, Dropbox only allowed a limited number of participants into the test phase. In the second phase, it generated a video which demonstrated the core features of the product: the cloud-based storage and the capability to share files. At this point there was no functioning product or prototype. The video alone attracted 75,000 early adopters. Dropbox received extensive feedback, which served above all to simplify and improve usability. They used a product called Votebox to establish a dialogue with customers about product features. Dropbox continue to use Votebox to this day, an electronic voting system based upon open source software, which has been used in research projects and even as a commercial voting system (VoteBox, n. d.). Subsequently, Dropbox increased their use of A/B tests to filter out the best solutions from multiple versions. Of particular interest is that Dropbox was an early implementer of personalised applications. When their system identified that a user didn't use particular features, Dropbox would send them information about it and its usefulness. Other users, who had used up their storage allocations, received e-mails with offers of additional storage for themselves and their friends. With strategies such as these, Dropbox quickly achieved high market penetration, direct and cheap customer feedback, and highly usable data about product use.

The enthusiasm of early adopters convinced the Dropbox developers to continue with their development. They asked themselves how could they increase the number of users. In response, Dropbox invested in classical marketing, which was not successful. After this, the company invested in a customer recommendation programme, in which new users and existing users who successfully recommended new users received free storage. Within 15 months, the user base grew from 100,000 to 4 million.

Advantages and Challenges

Dropbox is still committed to the basic principles of lean startup: building up a motivated user base, communicating regularly with users and allowing them a high degree of influence on the product direction. Traditional marketing does not play any part in customer relations. On the contrary, agile and cost-effective methods, rapid and ongoing improvements to the product and data-driven product decisions drive the development of the organisation.

INNOVATION PROCESS: GOOGLE DESIGN SPRINT

Google of course is the leader in Internet search. In 1997, the two founders from Stanford University put their search engine online under the name 'Google'. Because of the enormous success of the search capability, the organisation has been able to introduce many other products in areas such as communication, data management and analysis, and navigation. Fundamental to this strategy is that scalability, the ability to rapidly expand product adoption to very high levels, is a requirement of every potential

Google product or service. This strategy explains the intense development speed of the organisation. With Design Sprint, Google has established its own innovation process, which has since become a service available to other organisations.

A Design Sprint (Google, n. d.) consists of five phases (Knapp, Zeratsky, & Kowitz, 2016), which are usually executed in five days. The goal is to solve important problems with rapid prototyping and interaction with users or customers. In such Sprints, teams solve problems to achieve clearly defined goals and produce definite outcomes. At the core of a Design Sprint is the rapid learning achieved by the participating team. Being an innovation process, it is intended to result in new products, features and services, and so demands customer-oriented thinking. Furthermore, product development cycles are accelerated through team spirit and the growth of a common vision.

The Google Design Sprint came into being at Google by observing and learning from internal projects, elements of Design Thinking (Hasso-Plattner Institut, n. d.) methods and other customer-focused research methods as applied by IDEO (IDEO, n. d.) (a global design and innovation firm) or by Stanford's dschool (dschool, n. d.) in California (Fig. 10.2).

The five phases of the Google Design Sprint have been implemented under the leadership of Google by the Headspace Corporation.

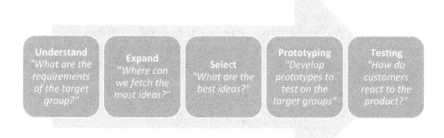

Fig. 10.2 Google's Design Sprint

Case Study: Headspace

Headspace executed a Google Design Sprint with the objective of winning new customers. Before beginning the process, the organisation had to define clear goals, such as new customer acquisition or growing market share. The specific challenge for Headspace was to take a product that successfully appealed to adults and make it attractive to children. Headspace helps people to acquire skills in meditation and mindfulness. As well as events and books, the main product is an app which contains aids to meditating and related tools. This has been downloaded 14 million times in 190 countries. Headspace has considered developing the product for children for some time, but this has been associated with considerable challenges; for example, children don't like to sit still. The objective was clear but the means of achieving it were not, so in 2016 Headspace executed a Google Design Sprint.

In the first step on the first day the firm tried, with the help of the 'Sprint Master', to find out the needs of children and their apps usage behaviour . They took as their model the YouTube for children app, and in this way developed an understanding for the new user group. The focus on days two and three moved to extending existing ideas. The team started with many questions, all beginning with 'How can we …' These were grouped into clusters and were subsequently used for the generation of ideas. By asking these questions, the space around possible solutions was outlined without solutions being produced too early. Question clusters were assigned to individuals or groups, who were removed from the group to draw up solutions and then brought back later into the full team. Next, the ideas were developed by the whole team. Session durations were fixed and tightly managed. At the conclusion of the third day it had been decided what needed to be developed. On the fourth day, a semi-functioning prototype was built in the form of an app. On the fifth and final day, the app was tested with selected users.

Advantages and Challenges

The team came to surprising conclusions. Headspace found it was indeed possible to get children to meditate, but concentrating for longer than a minute was difficult for them. Children are prepared to practise their mindfulness through meditation, but only for a brief period.

The team continued to work on the product and independently initiated a second Design Sprint in order to further develop the prototype. This product was brought quickly and smoothly onto the market. Further, the Design Sprint method spread throughout the organisation. Perhaps the most important outcome of the project was the recognition that a deep understanding of the target group is needed and that the immediate use of prototypes by this group can improve the product step by step. Headspace noticed that refined market research was unnecessary. A structured process with a varied customer set sufficed. The closeness to customers was internalised by the participating team members and supported future market-driven focused innovation.

INNOVATION PROCESS: THE HACKATHON

Even something that sounds as chaotic as a hackathon actually runs according to a clearly defined and repeatable pattern. An increasing number of firms, including Microsoft, Postbank, Zalando and Bosch, have copied this innovation process from the startup scene. The main object of a hackathon is often hardware or software development. They are limited in time to one or a few days (Frey & Luks, 2016). The process often begins with presentations or discussions, the purpose of which is to aid recognition of the problem and to provide a shared understanding for the participants. Following this, ideas and suggestions are collected which are explored by teams. These teams are of mixed backgrounds and skills and are usually self-selecting. Then the real work begins, taking hours or days to reach any form of presentable conclusion. Participants will often stay at the location, intensely working on ideas, even when the hackathon runs over many days. If the outcome is software, prototypes are often developed and presented. A hardware prototype might be a toy combined with a mobile device that can be shown with a theatrical backdrop to achieve a presentation effect. All prototypes are presented and are often evaluated by a jury. In some cases the winning team might win valuable prizes (including money) and useful contacts for the further development of their idea (Fig. 10.3).

Case Study: Deutsche Bahn

Established companies such as the Deutsche Bahn (German federal railway) use hackathons with external creatives as well as with their own

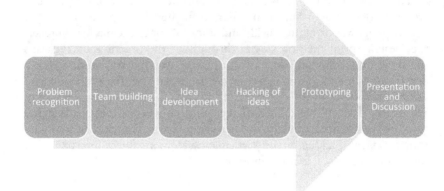

Fig. 10.3 The Hackathon process

employees. Working only with their own employees has the advantage of being able to use confidential data, when it would not be appropriate to share this with external parties. In 2016, Deutsch Bahn carried out Hackathons simultaneously in two locations for 24 hours with 100 employees grouped into 20 teams. The goal was to solve a variety of quite specific problems such as route optimisation. Of great importance was the fact that employees from diverse locations and departments could work on open data to develop innovative ideas and application proposals.

Advantages and Challenges

Organisations such as Deutsche Bahn use the process of hackathons not only to generate innovation, but also to introduce long-term culture change. Cooperation and network-building between diverse teams and employees is an important strategic goal. In the hackathons, not only did impressive ideas emerge, such as an Online Tracking System for rail transport of all kinds, the 'My Station' app (in which all information about the station, local businesses, schedules and carriage placement is available) and the mobile parking-space finder for commuters, customers or city visitors. Deutsche Bahn also encouraged the engagement of its own employees to think creatively and to feel that they are empowered and active members of the organisation. Furthermore, the composition of diverse teams from different locations and departments is an important driver of innovative solutions. The explicit team-building part of hackathons allows companies to bring different ideas and perspectives into one place.

INNOVATION PROCESS FROM SOFTWARE DEVELOPMENT: SCRUM

The concept of 'agile management' originated in project management, and is so formulated in order to contrast with classic, linear phase models of project organisation such as the waterfall model. In such models, a project is broken down into phases such as requirements, design, code and test: each phase produces certain outcomes which flow into the following phase. Such methods are generally rigid, do not allow for iteration and cope poorly with change (Vieweg, 2015): they are unsuitable for complex tasks and projects which have higher levels of uncertainty. Where requirements, solution technologies or market demands are dynamic, a predefined plan is often out of date before the ink has dried.

Agile methods, such as the scrum principle, are a departure from these highly-structured approaches. They recognise that many of the problems arising in large projects are in general a consequence of an inappropriate set of organising principles—they are not due to human or technological failure. This realisation led to the Agile Manifesto of 2001 (Agile Manifesto, n. d.). In this document it is stated that individuals and interactions are more important than processes and tools. Working software is more important than comprehensive documentation. Collaboration with customers is more important than contract negotiations, and responding to change is more important than following the plan.

Although initially only used in software development, agile methods have found their way into other industries. Instead of developing voluminous documents and specifications, projects work with a minimal set. The focus is on exploiting what is currently possible and on continuous communication with customers. Executable modules and usable systems are continuously tested for usability and function—bugs and errors in interpretation of requirements can thereby be corrected in a timely manner. Cooperative sprints and permanent exchanges between teams, usually conducted in brief daily stand-up meetings, and a shared team planning whiteboard create an environment of an iterative, dynamic and evolving process in which all stakeholders move towards a solution. The first step is

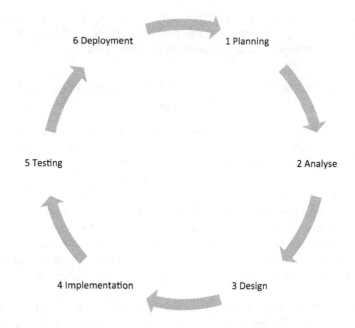

Fig. 10.4 Scrum: the step-by-step approach to resolve complex problems

planning, followed by analysis, design, implementation and test, and then customer use, this being followed by as many iterations as are required (Fig. 10.4).

Case Study: Scout 24

Scout 24 are based in Munich, and since 1998 they operate a variety of online marketplaces in various industries such as automobiles, finance and real estate. They do business in 18 countries and employ over 1800 people. In 2008 they were one of the first German organisations to introduce scrum into their information technology (IT) development, and since then it has expanded to cover all product development. In 2010, Scout 24, in collaboration with Immobilienscout 24, initiated its own accelerator programme 'You is Now'. Successful founders receive co-financing, access to co-working spaces and access to organisational experts in product development and marketing.

Since about 2008, Scout 24 has been experimenting with scrum methods and according to their own reports, they have been able to improve their development speed and product quality, as well as reduce the rate of defects. The company does not only involve developers in its scrum process: product managers, business developers, marketing and sales staff are also included. Scout 24 has appointed a Head of Agile and Lean Management in order to encourage and support the use of agile processes.

Advantages and Challenges

The greatest challenge in implementing scrum lies in changing the organisational culture. The basic idea of scrum is self-organisation by individuals and teams. This requires that every employee in the firm understands themselves to be part of a system and sees their tasks and activities as being connected to others: the need to collaborate, work across boundaries and communicate directly is a natural consequence of this view. It is important to specify and assign clearly defined roles such as 'scrum master' and 'team member'. Hierarchies become less important and managers and employees share open-plan offices. This may be challenging for organisations in which managers see themselves as deserving particular privileges, and the self-concept of leadership may need to change: the leader is more of a coach than a boss.

CONCLUSION

In this chapter we have presented a number of agile methods, but what do they have in common? Above all, and at their core, they provide ways of dealing with uncertainty and generating solutions to problems which are complex and poorly understood. This kind of complexity is not easy to draw boundaries around or reduce to a few simple principles. The kinds of solutions that might be suitable can often not be anticipated, and the problem situations can be paradoxical and characterised by contradictions in how participants view the issues. Involvement of stakeholders at all levels, critical open-mindedness, evolutionary resolution and prototyping, and rapid feedback reveal more about the problem situation and are more suitable than deterministic approaches which try and develop finished models from an uncertain base. An honest recognition of ignorance and uncertainty invites the use of the kind of principles espoused by these approaches, and the use of agile methods is increasing.

Established companies can use these methods to prepare themselves for innovation and a digital future. To summarise, the methods we have discussed are characterised by:

- low entry costs,
- rapid changes in the direction of development,
- intensive use of customer feedback for continuous improvement to products and services,
- rapid development of prototypes and in-flight products,
- use of the Internet and digital media for data collection and analysis and for customer testing,
- deep, specific and practical customer feedback instead of broad, shallow and predefined market research.

The application of these methods supports organisations in generating successful innovations in complex and uncertain environments; but implementation may require a fundamental cultural change throughout the firm.

<h2 style="text-align:center">REFERENCES</h2>

Agile Manifesto. (n. d.). *Manifesto for Agile software development.* Retrieved from http://agilemanifesto.org/

Business.com. (n. d.). *The Dropbox effect: How to utilize the lean startup methodology.* Retrieved from https://www.business.com/articles/how-to-utilize-the-lean-startup-methodoly/?q=dropbox

dschool. (n. d.). *Explore the Stanford d.school.* Retrieved from https://dschool.stanford.edu/

Frey, F. J., & Luks, M. (2016). *The innovation-driven hackathon: One means for accelerating innovation.* In Proceedings of the 21st European Conference on Pattern Languages of Programs (p. 10). ACM.

Google. (n. d.). *Headspace explores a new audience.* Retrieved from https://designsprintkit.withgoogle.com/case-studies/headspace-explores-a-new-audience/

Hasso-Plattner-Institut. (n. d.). *Thinking new, working differently.* Retrieved from https://hpi.de/en/school-of-design-thinking/design-thinking.html

IDEO. (n. d.). *Work blog tools.* Retrieved from https://www.ideo.com/eu

Knapp, J., Zeratsky, J., & Kowitz, B. (2016). *Sprint: How to solve big problems and test new ideas in just five days.* New York: Simon and Schuster.

Ries, E. (2014). *Lean startup: Schnell, risikolos und erfolgreich Unternehmen gründen.* München: Redline Wirtschaft.

Vieweg, W. (2015). *Management in Komplexität und Unsicherheit.* Wiesbaden, Germany: Springer Essentials.

VoteBox. (n. d.). *WHAT IS VOTEBOX?* Retrieved from: http://votebox.cs.rice.edu/

Index[1]

[1] Note: Page numbers followed by 'n' refer to notes.

© The Author(s) 2018
N. Richter et al. (eds.), *Entrepreneurial Innovation and Leadership*,
https://doi.org/10.1007/978-3-319-71737-1

GPSR Compliance
The European Union's (EU) General Product Safety Regulation (GPSR) is a set
of rules that requires consumer products to be safe and our obligations to
ensure this.

If you have any concerns about our products, you can contact us on

ProductSafety@springernature.com

In case Publisher is established outside the EU, the EU authorized
representative is:

Springer Nature Customer Service Center GmbH
Europaplatz 3
69115 Heidelberg, Germany